# Intermediate Access

## ACCESS ESSENTIALS BOOK 2

M.L. HUMPHREY

ISBN: 978-1-950902-92-7

# SELECT TITLES BY M.L. HUMPHREY

**ACCESS ESSENTIALS**
Access for Beginners
Intermediate Access

**EXCEL ESSENTIALS**
Excel for Beginners
Intermediate Excel
50 Useful Excel Functions
50 More Excel Functions

**WORD ESSENTIALS**
Word for Beginners
Intermediate Word

**POWERPOINT ESSENTIALS**
PowerPoint for Beginners
Intermediate PowerPoint

**BUDGETING FOR BEGINNERS**
Budgeting for Beginners
Excel for Budgeting

# CONTENTS

# INTRODUCTION

This book continues from where *Access for Beginners* left off. In *Access for Beginners* we walked through the four main components of an Access database, covered the basics of working within each of those components and in Access in general, discussed how to create a table either from scratch or by uploading an Excel or .csv file, and then covered how to create a basic select query using one or multiple data sources.

But there was a lot that wasn't covered in that book because Access is a very complicated program with a wide range of capabilities. So this book continues where the last one left off. Here we will cover how to add default values to tables, how to add validation rules to tables, how to add a fixed field to a query, how to add a calculated field to a query, how to create union queries, crosstab queries, and parameter queries, and also how to customize the content and formatting of reports and forms.

That still won't cover all of Access's capabilities, but by the time we're done here you should be comfortably able to work in Access on a day-to-day basis.

Now keep in mind here that I come to Access as an Excel user who needed more capability than Excel could give me and that from my perspective there are two main reasons to use Access.

One, to create a database that allows you to combine information from different sources into summary reports. (In my case, I have an Access database that combines information from multiple vendors and provides summary reports related to my books and videos.)

Two, when dealing with data that includes entries that contain significant amounts of text. If you're working with those types of entries you'll find that at some point Excel requires manual adjustment of your row height to display the full text of a cell and even then sometimes doesn't do so. Using forms in Access can be a far better solution in that case.

As I mentioned in *Access for Beginners*, I think there are probably far better solutions out there these days for a number of the ways Access may have been used in the past, which means that I probably will not cover in these two books ways to use Access that are of interest to database developers.

For example, I'm not going to cover how to run a delete query, because I think if you need one you need a product other than Access. And I'm not going to dig into how to use SQL in Access at more than a very cursory level of detail. (It comes up with adding a union query, but I suspect there are certain Access users who only use SQL to build their queries and that's not the target audience for this book.)

This book is targeting Excel users who want to be able to learn Access. And it is written as a continuation of *Access for Beginners*.

Also, this book is written using Access 2013. I believe the general principles of how to do everything we're going to discuss here should be the same for any version of Access from Access 2007 onward, but there may be times that things look a little different or work in a slightly different way if you're using a different version of Access.

This book is about what is possible as much as it is about the mechanics of how to do it. As long as you know something is possible you can find the way to do it in a newer version. It's usually working backwards to an older version that presents more of a challenge because sometimes the developers add new bells and whistles to a new version that don't exist in older ones. But I don't think what we're covering here falls under that heading.

Okay.

So there you have it. I'm going to briefly cover basic terminology and the four components of an Access database as a review, and then we'll dive in on adding default values to a table.

# BASIC TERMINOLOGY RECAP

All of these terms were already covered in *Access for Beginners*, so I'm going to walk through them again here but in far less detail and without any screenshots.

## Tab

I refer to the menu choices at the top of the screen (File, Home, Create, External Data, Database Tools, etc.) as tabs. Each tab you select will show you different options.

## Click

If I tell you to click on something, that means to use your mouse (or trackpad) to move the cursor over to a specific location and left-click or right-click on the option. (See the next definition for the difference between left-click and right-click).

## Left-click/Right-click

If you look at your mouse or your trackpad, you generally have two flat buttons to press. One is on the left side, one is on the right. If I say left-click that means to press down on the button on the left. If I say right-click that means press down on the button on the right.

## Dropdown Menu

If you right-click on something in Access, for example a field or table name, you will see what I'm going to refer to as a dropdown menu. A dropdown menu provides you a list of choices to select from.

## Dialogue Box

Dialogue boxes are pop-up boxes that cover specialized settings.

## Panes

Panes are task areas that are separate from the main workspace. For example, the All Access Objects pane is on the left-hand side of the workspace by default.

## Scroll Bar

Scroll bars allow you to see your data when there is sufficient data to take up more space than is currently available on the screen. They are visible on the right-hand side or bottom of the pane, workspace, or field listing when needed.

## Arrow

If I ever tell you to arrow to the left or right or up or down, that just means use your arrow keys.

## Tab Through or Tab To

I may instead tell you to tab through or tab to your data. This is different from the tabs we discussed above. In this instance, we're talking about using the Tab key to move right or the Shift and Tab key together to move left.

## Table

There are actually two different types of tables I talk about in Access.

One is one of the four main components of an Access database where your imported or input data is stored.

The other is how data appears in Datasheet View for both tables and queries.

## Column/Field

Every table in Access consists of rows and columns of information. Columns, which can also be referred to as fields, run across the top of the workspace and are named Field1, Field2, etc. by default.

## Row/Record

Rows/records run downward in a data table.

You should think of each row of a data table in Access as containing a related set of information that will always stay together. Technically, this is best referred to as a record.

## Cell or Entry or Value

When I refer to a cell in Access I am referring to the intersection of a column and row.

It is probably more appropriate to refer to values or entries but in a generic sense I will still say something like, "click into the cell next to the cell that contains the value you want to copy."

## Control Shortcuts

In Access there are various control shortcuts that you can use to perform tasks like save, copy, cut, and paste.

Each time I refer to one it will be written as Ctrl + a capital letter, such as Ctrl + C which will copy a selection and means to hold down the Ctrl key and the c key at the same time.

## Undo

Access does have an Undo option which will generally let you undo your last action. It's available in the Quick Access Toolbar in the top left corner of the screen or by using Ctrl + Z. But don't rely on it. Not everything in Access can be undone.

# OVERVIEW OF THE FOUR MAIN COMPONENTS OF AN ACCESS DATABASE

As discussed in *Access for Beginners*, I break Access down into four main components: Tables, Queries, Forms, and Reports. Each component (object type) is shown by default in its own section in the All Access Objects pane.

## Tables

Tables are the bedrock upon which everything else is built. This is where all of your data is actually kept.

It is up to the user(s) of the Access database to define what columns of data are in each table and provide the values that go into each record.

## Queries

Queries are where you tell Access how to pull together the information in your various data tables or from other queries. They are where the bulk of the analysis is done. Your tables are the raw material, your queries are where you put that material together to make something useful.

## Forms

Forms allow you to display each record from a table in a more user-friendly way. If you're doing direct data entry into your Access database (something I would caution against), they can be easier to work in than tables. An edit to an entry in a form is recorded in its associated table.

The default format for a form is one record per page, but this can be changed.

## Reports

Reports take the information you have in a table or query and they put it in a report format that has better formatting for print or distribution.

* * *

Okay, now that we've reviewed the basics from *Access for Beginners*, let's talk about how to use default values and how to include data validation in tables.

# TABLES:
## DEFAULT VALUES

I don't use default values in my Access databases because I usually upload all of the information in my tables from other sources. But if you are entering data directly into Access you may want to set a field to a default value.

I would only do this if you have fields in your table that are 95% of the time a single value. So, for me for example, if I had a field that said whether an item was a book, an audiobook, a video, or a template I might set that to book as a default because the large majority of what I publish are books.

So let's walk through how to do this.

Open in Design View the table with the field where you want to set a default value.

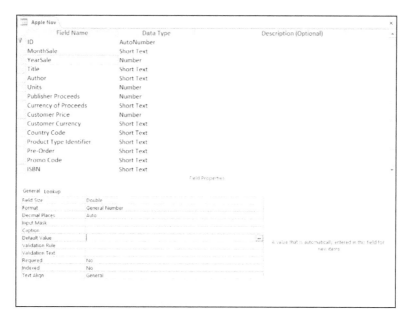

Click on the field name in the top portion of the screen. Above I've clicked on YearSale.

Now, look in the Field Properties section at the bottom of the screen.

About five lines down you should see a line that says "Default Value". Enter there the default value that you want for that field.

Keep in mind that the default value must match the field data type. So you can't set a default value of "fifty" in a field that has a data type of Number. (If you do that, Access will assume you're trying to reference the value in another field and will put it in brackets and then generate an error message when you try to return to Datasheet View.)

Also, you can't set a default value for any primary key field or the Access ID field since those have to be unique values.

Here I've entered a default value of 2020 for the field:

| General  Lookup | |
|---|---|
| Field Size | Double |
| Format | General Number |
| Decimal Places | Auto |
| Input Mask | |
| Caption | |
| Default Value | 2020 ←———— **Default Value** ... |
| Validation Rule | |
| Validation Text | |
| Required | No |
| Indexed | No |
| Text Align | General |

After you've set your default value, save your changes to the table with Ctrl + S or by clicking on the save icon in the Quick Access Toolbar in the top left corner.

Return to Datasheet View. (If you forgot to save, Access will prompt you to save the changes to the table.)

You'll now see that your default value is already showing in the last row of your table where you would enter your next record.

Here it is for the 2020 value I added to YearSale. You can see it's a new record because the ID is currently shown as (New):

| ID | MonthSale | YearSale | Title | Author |
|---|---|---|---|---|
| 1 | November | 2018 | Title1 Is Really F | Author1 |
| 2 | November | 2019 | Title1 | Author1 |
| 3 | November | 2019 | Title1 | Author1 |
| 4 | November | 2019 | Title1 | Author1 |
| 5 | November | 2018 | Title2 | Author2 |
| 6 | November | 2019 | Title2 | Author2 |
| 7 | November | 2019 | Title2 | Author2 |
| 8 | November | 2019 | Title3 | Author1 |
| * (New) | | 2020 ←———— | | |

\* \* \*

You don't just have to add fixed values for a default value.

Typing Date() into the field will provide today's date. Typing =Date()+10 will give a date ten days from now. Etc.

Also, if you're using text for your default value you should put quotation marks around the text, especially if there is any sort of punctuation involved. This lets Access know it's a fixed text entry and not a field reference. So, "January" would put January into each new record for that field.

# TABLES:
## VALIDATION RULES

Another trick to use in Access if you're inputting data is to include a validation rule for a field. Access automatically runs certain validation rules against input values based on the field type. So you can't enter "fifty" for a Number field, for example. Or it will convert 1.2345 to 1 in a Number field set to Integer.

But you still may want to add further constraints to a field. For example, in my YearSale field, there should never be a value that isn't in the 2000s. So 2020 is fine, but 1920 or 20200 is not.

To add a validation rule to a field, open your table and go to Design View.

In the top section click on the field where you want to add validation, and then go down to the Field Properties section at the bottom.

About the sixth row down will be for Validation Rule.

Add your requirements for the field here.

If you're familiar with Excel, the way to write a rule here is basically the same as how you'd write a formula in Excel. You can use the numeric operators (>, <, <>, =, etc.) as well as AND and OR. You can also use wildcard characters for text like the asterisk (*) and the question mark (?).

In the example I just gave above about limited my year of sale to something in the 2000s what rule I used would depend on how the field was formatted.

If the field was formatted as text I could use, "Like 20??" where each of the question marks is a wildcard standing in for one character. Of course, that would also allow something like 20AS. It wouldn't be limited to numeric values.

If the field was formatted as a number I could use, >1999 AND <2100, where the less than and greater than signs set my value range.

(Just be careful if you're using AND that you don't set criteria that are mutually exclusive so make it impossible to enter any value. If I did >1999 AND <2000 and I'm only allowing whole numbers in that field, there's nothing that would satisfy both.)

In the next row down, Validation Text, you can also add a message that will display if someone enters a wrong value.

Here is an example for the YearSale field when it's a Number data type where I've specified that the value must be greater than 1999 and less than 2100 and set a message to say, "Year must be between 2000 and 2099."

| General Lookup | |
|---|---|
| Field Size | Double |
| Format | General Number |
| Decimal Places | Auto |
| Input Mask | |
| Caption | **Validation Rule and Text** |
| Default Value | |
| Validation Rule | >1999 And <2100 |
| Validation Text | Year Must Be Between 2000 and 2099 |
| Required | No |
| Indexed | No |
| Text Align | General |

\* \* \*

As with default values, you will need to save your changes before you can return to Datasheet View.

Also, when you do that, Access is going to tell you that your data integrity rules have been changed and will confirm that you really wanted to do that. It will also ask you whether you want it to run the rules against your old data.

Ideally, the answer there is yes that you do want to run the rules against your old data because why have rules in place if they don't apply to part of your data. However, if you already have a lot of values in your table that can take a significant amount of time.

If you do have an entry in your existing table that doesn't fit your validation rule, Access will tell you that existing data violates the new setting and ask if you want to keep going.

If you say yes to continuing, Access will still keep that old value in the table and won't flag that record for you in any way. You'll just know that it exists somewhere in your table.

\* \* \*

Once you're back in Datasheet View, if you have a validation rule in place and you enter a value that doesn't work, Access will show an error dialogue box with the message you provided under Validation Text and require that you change the value until it does meet your rule or delete the value.

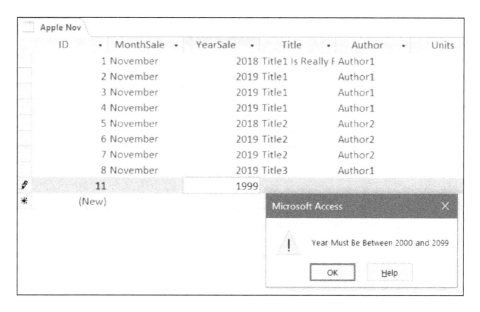

\* \* \*

Another sort of validation is to require that a field be completed for any new record. To do this, go to the Design View, click on that field, and in the Field Properties section change the value next to Required to Yes.

\* \* \*

Now let's talk about how to include a fixed value in a query.

# QUERIES:
## INCLUDING A FIXED VALUE IN A QUERY

One of my summary queries in my Access database is a union query, which we'll discuss in a minute. It takes all of my ebook sales from all of my different platforms and combines them into one single query.

When I built that query I didn't want to lose who the original vendor was for each of my sales. I still wanted to be able to look at the final query and ask, "How much have I made from ebook sales on Apple for this title?" or "On Google?"

Each of my queries that ties to a vendor table is named with that vendor name, so I can always open the original queries to see those values. But I wanted to have a column in my final query that showed the vendor name so that I could just go to that one query and filter on that vendor name and have my answer.

To do that, I had to add a fixed value to my query. A new column/field that would list the vendor name.

I originally learned how to do this in SQL View. (For those who know SQL, you basically add a new field to the SELECT portion of the query. Put the value you want to repeat in single quotes, follow that with AS, and follow that with the field name you want. So, 'Nook' AS Vendor, will give you a field labeled Vendor where all entries are "Nook".)

But after I learned how to do it in SQL View, I realized that it was incredibly easy to do in Design View. So that's the method I'm going to teach you here. All you need is the column/field name you want to use and the value you want to show in that column/field.

So. Open your query where you want to add your fixed value and go to Design View.

Go to the next available field in the bottom section where you can see your selected columns, and in the top row, type your chosen field name, then a colon, and then in single quotes the value you want shown in each entry for that column. So, Vendor: 'Nook', for example.

Here is a query in Design View where I have added a fifth column to include a field name Vendor with a value of "Nook":

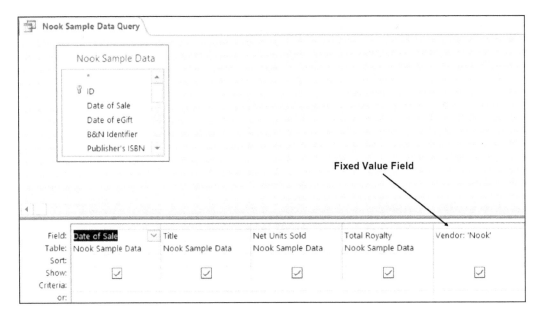

Here's how that looks in Datasheet View:

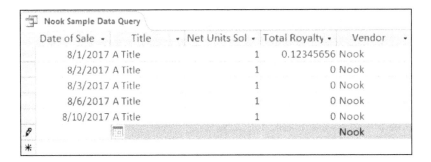

There you have it. It's that easy to add a column with a fixed value to a query. Just name, colon, and then single quotes around the value you want for text. (If you want a fixed number value, just type the number value, no need for the single quotes.

Be sure to save the changes to your query when you close it to keep your fixed field value.

# QUERIES:
# WRITING A SIMPLE CALCULATION INTO A QUERY

Now let's discuss how to include a calculation in a query.

I tend to use the Builder which is located under the Query Setup section of the Design tab under Query Tools when you have a query open in Design View.

But the reason I'm covering this now is that you really don't have to do that. You can actually write your formula right there under Field Name. And it's not that different from including a fixed value.

The only difference is that you reference other field names instead of fixed text, and use basic notation to indicate addition, subtraction, multiplication, and division.

A plus sign (+) stands for add. A minus sign (–) stands for subtract. A star (*) stands for multiply. And a forward slash (/) stands for divide.

(If you know how to write formulas in Excel, it's basically the same.)

To reference field names, if the field name is all one word, you can just write it out. But if the field name has spaces in it, you need to use brackets around the name.

So, the field name Title can be left as Title, but the field name Total Royalty needs to be written as [Total Royalty].

Let's do an example. Here is a basic table of data in Design View:

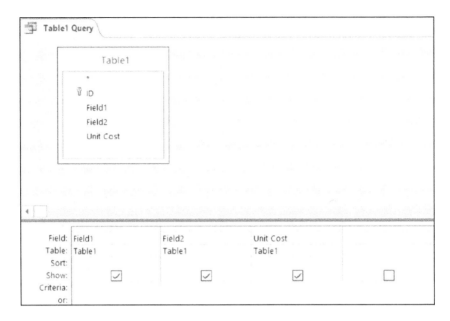

Let's say I want to multiply Units by Unit Cost and call it Total Cost.

I can write that in a new column in the Field row as:

Total Cost:Units*[Unit Cost]

The portion of the text on the left-hand side of the colon is the field name I want to use, in this case Total Cost.

The portion of the text on the right-hand side of the colon is my expression/equation. In this case, the field Units multiplied by the field Unit Cost. I've put brackets around Unit Cost since there is a space in the field name. I could just as easily put brackets around Units, but I don't have to.

We do that, return to Datasheet View and what we get is this:

| Field1 | Units | Unit Cost | Total Cost |
|--------|-------|-----------|------------|
| Data | 2 | 1.25 | 2.5 |
| test | 3 | 2.5 | 7.5 |
| other | 1 | 1.5 | 1.5 |
| Test | 0 | 1 | 0 |

We now have a new column in the query called Total Cost and it is showing the result of multiplying the Units field by the Unit Cost field for each row.

In this case, that's all that needed to be done. With some queries, especially ones that work with multiple tables or summarize values, you also need to make sure that the Total row for that field is set to Expression.

Here is an example where the final field is calculating Revenue Per Unit by dividing Proceeds by Units:

| Field: | Title | Units: Units | Proceeds: Publisher Proceeds | Rev per Unit: [Proceeds]/[Units] |
|---|---|---|---|---|
| Table: | Ebook Link Table | Apple Nov | Apple Nov | |
| Total: | Group By | Sum | Sum | Expression |
| Sort: | | | | |
| Show: | ☑ | ☑ | ☑ | ☑ |
| Criteria: | | | | |
| or: | | | | |

See how the Total row has been set to Expression. I find I need to make this change fairly often when I'm adding new calculations, so if you add a new calculation and it isn't working, check for that.

\* \* \*

The examples above were numeric equations. But just like in Excel you can also write expressions in Access that combine the values in different text fields and can make combinations of text fields with fixed values.

This is done using the ampersand (&) and quotation marks around any fixed text you want. So,

TitleByAuthor: [Apple Nov]![Title] & " by " & [Author]

would return for me a field named TitleByAuthor with the text "Title by Author" in it where the values for Title and Author were pulled from their respective fields and combined with fixed text that is a space and then the word by and then another space.

When working with text that you're bringing together like this you need to tell Access every single space or punctuation mark you want to use. If you don't it will just smoosh all of your different text fields together. So that " by " portion is necessary and needs to have those spaces included on both sides for the final value to display properly.

Also, you'll note above that we have [Apple Nov]![Title] instead of just Title. This is because in this case I was dealing with a query that had two tables in it, both of which used the field name Title. I had to tell Access which table to pull from, Apple Nov by including it in my expression. The brackets are there because it's a table name with a space in it. The exclamation mark between the table name and the field name tells Access this is a table and this is a field in that table.

One final note. In this case, the expression only worked for me if I left the field as a Group By field, perhaps because it was text values.

\* \* \*

Okay.

So as I showed you, you can type your equation right there in the field row itself, but when I'm writing a more complex equation than FieldA + FieldB, I find it can get very messy very fast. And while I know I can change the column width to make more of my text visible, I usually just work in the Builder instead because it also saves me from typing in a field name wrong.

Let's walk through how to do that.

First, open your query in Design View and click into the Field row of a blank column.

Now click on Builder. The Builder is located in the Query Setup section of the Design tab under Query Tools. When you open a query you should already be on this tab and be able to see it.

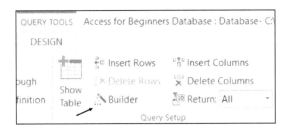

This will bring up the Expression Builder dialogue box:

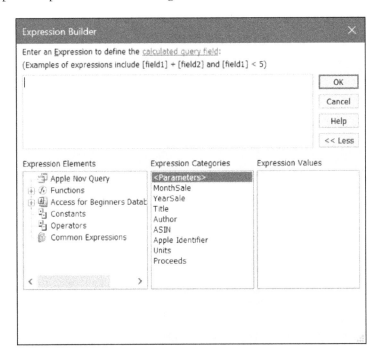

The white space at the top is where you can build your equation.

Expression Elements on the left-hand side allows you to navigate to any field in a table or query. It also shows your expression building elements.

Expression Categories in the center shows the fields that are available to you in your currently-selected object.

Expression Values shows more detailed values when they exist.

\* \* \*

Going back to Expression Elements, your current query will show at the top of the list. If you click on the plus sign next to your database name, which is generally third in the row, you'll be able to see all of your Access objects types. Clicking on the plus sign next to an object type (e.g., table) will show all of your objects of that type that currently exist in the database. Clicking on the name of one of those will show you the fields available to you in the Expression Categories section.

So here I've chosen Tables and then Apple Nov:

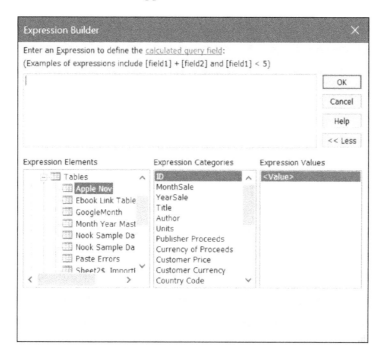

Selecting field through the database navigation option in the Builder makes sure that the table name is properly referenced in your formula. If you just select your fields from your table as they're listed in the default view in the Builder they'll be added in without the table/query reference, which may be an issue. (Or may not.) It all depends on if you have multiple inputs to your query that use the same field name.

* * *

The Expression Elements section also lets you see the available Operators (like *, /, +, etc.), Constants (like False, Null, True), and Functions that you can use to build an expression. I tend not to use them that way, because there's no help that tells you what any of them mean so you already have to know what you're doing to use them, but it can be a good place to look if you're trying to figure out if something is available to you in Access.

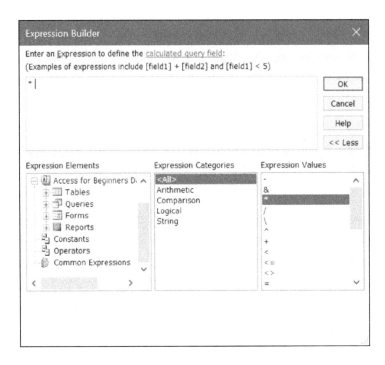

Just double-click on the input you want from Expression Values to add it to your workspace.

* * *

To build your equation/expression, you can just start building it right away. If you do that and don't include a field name your field will be assigned a name like Expr1 when you exit the builder. It's easy enough to change after the fact, but if you already know what you want to call the field you can start in the workspace by typing your name followed by a colon.

Next, choose your first field. Just double-click on the field name in Expression Categories. Sometimes Access will try to be helpful and add an <<Expr>> before the field name. If you weren't looking to use a function, like SUM, then just delete that and continue building your expression.

When you're done, click on OK and Access will take you back to the Design View where you can see your new field added to the list of fields.

* * *

Here is an example of a more complex formula to show why it's easier to work in the Builder rather than directly in a field:

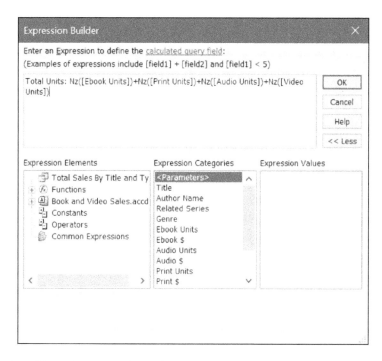

In this example, I'm adding the values from four separate columns in the query together. Far easier to build this in the Builder where I can see all of that at once than in the field cell where I'd be limited in what I could see and be trying to get each field name right. (And before I had simplified my field names and the fields were called things like SumOfSumOfUnits, it was far, far easier to work in Builder than try to type that in myself directly in Design View.)

Alright. Now let's talk about troubleshooting some issues with expressions.

# QUERIES:
# TROUBLESHOOTING ISSUES WITH EXPRESSIONS

If you look at the screenshot above you'll see that I've placed an Nz() around each of the values I want to add together. The equation I used is:

Nz([Ebook Units])+Nz([Print Units])+Nz([Audio Units])+Nz([Video Units])

The reason I did that is because I found when I was first building my database that when I tried to add multiple items together that Access wouldn't return a result for a specific record unless it had a value for each of the items I was trying to add.

So in the example above I want the total number of units for a title that have been sold in ebook, print, audio, and video. But all of my titles that are in audio are not in video and vice versa and many that are in ebook or print are in neither audio nor video. The use of the Nz() around each value lets Access still add the results from the other categories without being stopped by the fact that there's a null value in one of my categories.

Now, you may not have this issue, depending on how your data is set up. For example, I have this issue with respect to my video units which show blank lines when there hasn't been a sale of that title, but not with respect to my audio units which show a value of zero when there hasn't been a sale.

So I'm sure this issue could also be fixed somewhere in the data input or data upload process, but I just find it easier to use Nz() and not have to worry about it.

\* \* \*

Another issue you may encounter is the Enter Parameter Value dialogue box:

We'll talk later about how to deliberately generate one of these dialogue boxes, but I've found that they also show up when I have a misnamed field somewhere. Basically, Access is looking for a value in a field, can't find it, so asks the user to provide it.

I mentioned in *Access for Beginners* that as I was writing these books I decided to rename all of my fields to get rid of that "Sum of Sum of Net Units Sold" that Access likes to create. I replaced all of those field names with more sensible names like "Units". But that broke some of my reports which were still trying to find values using the old field names. (This happened in the summary rows in my reports. The detailed data fields were fine but any field that summed those values had to be replaced.)

To fix this, open the query or report that is requesting that parameter in Design View, figure out where a field with that name is being used, and replace that field name with the correct one. This may require you to go back to another table or query to fix the issue.

For example, if I have a query that pulls in results from another query, then even odds are that the field name that isn't working is in that original query not my new one.

For me with my reports when I changed the field names and this happened, I had to delete the summary fields and regenerate them. (Far easier than trying to edit the summary formula.)

Bottom line on this one, if you see one of these boxes and aren't expecting it, your query or report is pointing to something that doesn't exist and you should fix that. (I will note here that I have had queries that generate correct results even with one of these boxes popping up. I just hit enter when I saw it each time. But better to fix the issue.)

\* \* \*

That brings up something I touched on briefly in *Access for Beginners* but want to touch on again here. As we covered there, you can designate a field name using the colon. So Units: Sum of Units Sold will name a field Units.

Access is pretty good at carrying through that change to other queries or reports. If, however, you already used that field in an expression in that specific query before you made the name change, then when you change the name and try to go to Datasheet View, Access will generate an error message that you have an expression with invalid syntax.

It also won't let you close the query without fixing the issue. You will need to either change the field name back or go fix all references to that field name in any expressions in your current query.

\* \* \*

Another time I've seen that invalid syntax error message appear is when I was editing an expression that I'd written in Access and I accidentally dropped a paren or a bracket. If Access can figure out that you dropped a bracket it will tell you, but for complex equations it just knows that things don't match up.

So if you were working on an expression right before this error appeared, go back and walk through your formula and confirm that all opening parens have a matching closing paren and that all opening brackets have a matching closing bracket.

\* \* \*

Another one I mentioned briefly in *Access for Beginners* is that I have on occasion run into situations where Access was double-counting or even triple-counting a value when I combined multiple tables or queries. One solution I've found that works in those scenarios has been to change the option in the Total row in Design View from Sum to Max. This may not work all the time, but it's worth trying.

\* \* \*

Another I've run into when trying to build an expression was if there were two or more tables involved that used the same field name. For example, Title. In that case you need to make sure that you're specifying which table to pull that field from.

You can write it like the example in the last chapter where we had:

[Apple Nov]![Title]

Where the [Apple Nov]! portion was referencing the table where the field is located.

Your other option if you don't want to remember how to do that is to go into the Builder and select your fields from the Expression Elements section under your database name.

\* \* \*

One final issue to be aware of is, of course, relationships. If you're pulling data from more than one table or query and you haven't established a relationship between those tables/queries that will generate an error message. Access doesn't know how to link various sources of information unless you tell it how to do so.

\* \* \*

You will probably run into other errors along the way. My advice is to step back and think about what you were doing and then go through step-by-step to make sure everything is working the way you think it should. Check for parens, brackets, colons, etc. and make sure they're all in the right place. If you typed in field names, check that they're correct. Make sure your data types are the right ones for that type of expression. And make sure the operators (+, -, etc.) that you use are correct. And always, always double-check your results at the end and ask if they make sense.

# QUERIES: A SQL CRASH COURSE

Next I want to talk about Union Queries, but in order to do that we need to take a quick crash course in SQL. Basically, everything we've been doing so far has been working with a pretty little interface that makes what's really going on user-friendly to people like me who aren't computer programmers and don't want to work directly in SQL to make things happen.

But behind the scenes, all of those queries we're building are being run with SQL, which is a programming language that's pretty common.

For every query you build there is a corresponding SQL statement. To see that statement, simply choose SQL View from the View dropdown when you're in a query. You'll see something like this for a basic select query that's not doing any summations:

Or something like this for a more complex query that involves multiple tables and groups the data by specified fields:

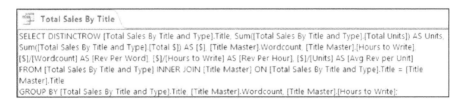

Let's take a quick step back and talk about what that SQL View is doing. That first image above is of a SQL statement for a query with four columns of data pulled from a single data source.

What that text says is:

> SELECT [Nook Sample Data].[Date of Sale], [Nook Sample Data].Title, [Nook Sample Data].[Net Units Sold], [Nook Sample Data].[Total Royalty]

FROM [Nook Sample Data];

Let's break that down.

The first word, SELECT, is telling Access to go get certain information.

The next part, [Nook Sample Data].[Date of Sale], is saying to go to the table named Nook Sample Data and pull in the field named Date of Sale.

Then we have, [Nook Sample Data].Title, which is doing the exact same thing except asking for the field named Title. (Remember that we don't need brackets when dealing with a single word.)

After that it's the same thing to pull Net Units Sold and Total Royalty.

Next we tell Access where to pull it from using the FROM clause. So, in this case, from Nook Sample Data.

The wording above is how Access wrote the query when I used the Query Wizard to create that query.

But, there's some duplicate information in there. This works just as well:

Now we have:

SELECT [Date of Sale], Title, [Net Units Sold], [Total Royalty]

FROM [Nook Sample Data];

Because we had the FROM clause that already said what table to pull those four fields from and were only using that one table, we really didn't need to repeat the table name each time in the SELECT row, too. (I suspect Access does this because you can have queries with multiple tables as the source and then that would matter in the SELECT portion of the query text.)

Okay.

So getting back to understanding this. What the SQL View is doing is showing you the computer language that is visually represented in the Design View. But the SQL View is the actual instructions. The Design View is just a pretty interface that makes it easier for people like me to work in Access without having to learn SQL.

Let's now walk through that more complex query. Here it is:

SELECT DISTINCTROW [Total Sales By Title and Type].Title, Sum([Total Sales By Title and Type].[Total Units]) AS Units, Sum([Total Sales By Title and Type].[Total $]) AS [$], [Title Master].Wordcount, [Title Master].[Hours to Write], [$]/[Wordcount] AS [Rev Per Word], [$]/[Hours to Write] AS [Rev Per Hour], [$]/[Units] AS [Avg Rev per Unit]

FROM [Total Sales By Title and Type] INNER JOIN [Title Master] ON [Total Sales By Title and Type].Title = [Title Master].Title

> GROUP BY [Total Sales By Title and Type].Title, [Title Master].Wordcount, [Title Master].[Hours to Write];

We already talked about SELECT. That's the first step. So Access is being told to go to each of those tables and select the values in those specific fields from each table.

The first one listed is pulling from a table called Total Sales by Title and Type and is pulling a field called Title.

The last entry, [$]/[Units] AS [Avg Rev per Unit], is telling Access to perform a calculation right there in that column using the $ and the Units fields that were created earlier in the query and telling Access to call that field Avg Rev per Unit.

That's what AS does. It tells Access what to name a field.

We also have a more complex FROM section in this query, because this one includes multiple tables.

> FROM [Total Sales By Title and Type] INNER JOIN [Title Master] ON [Total Sales By Title and Type].Title = [Title Master].Title

That's saying to join the Total Sales By Title and Type table/query to the Title Master table/query based on the value in the Title field of each one.

(Note that Access doesn't distinguish between tables and queries in the SQL View or in the Design View. To Access it's just information to be pulled into the current query.)

Finally, we have a new task that Access is performing called GROUP BY.

> GROUP BY [Total Sales By Title and Type].Title, [Title Master].Wordcount, [Title Master].[Hours to Write];

In this line Access is taking the raw data that would have listed all of the specified entries on a line-by-line basis and is now summarizing those values by grouping them according to the Title, Wordcount, and Hours to Write.

(The only one of which actually matters to me is Title, but that's how it's done for fields you aren't using for calculations.)

And then, so SQL can know it's done, the query ends with a semi-colon (;).

* * *

Kinda crazy, huh?

If it's the first time you've run across SQL that probably felt like drinking from a firehose. And you can forget most of it.

Because the key pieces of information you need to take away from everything we just discussed is:

That the SELECT portion of a query is where you tell Access what fields to include in the query. The order you list them in is the order in which they'll appear in your data table.

And that for any query you can copy that language from the SQL view and it will recreate the query wherever you paste that information.

Also that using a semi-colon tells Access to stop so you only want one of those and you want it at the end.

* * *

There is far more to SQL than what we just covered. Microsoft has some good overviews on their website and I'd suspect that a lot of programmer-types probably work almost exclusively in SQL when they work with Access, but for our purposes this is where we'll stop.

# QUERIES:
# UNION QUERIES

There was a point in time when I wanted to know what my total sales were across all of my different vendors. At the time the only way I could think to combine my reports from each vendor was using something called an Append Query. You basically run that type of query and it adds (or appends) your data onto the end of a data table you've established for that purpose. But the problem was I had to run each append query for each vendor separately. So every month I was having to sit there and run twelve different queries to get my information.

It was very time-consuming. And when I found sales that were missing, I had to rerun the whole thing. (Until I figured out how to add a fixed variable and then I just had to rerun the vendor with the missing info.)

Still. It was a lot of wasted effort. So I went in search of a different solution and discovered the beauty of union queries.

All I had to do with a union query was create it once and I had my data combined into one report just like that. So I love union queries. They are wonderful.

What exactly does a union query do? It essentially takes the results from various queries and stacks them on top of each other. The queries that you stack don't have to be tied to one another by any sort of relationship. Ideally, what you should have is the same information in the same order in each one so that it makes sense to stack the results, but that's not even required.

Union queries are built using SQL, which is why we did our crash course above because it's good to be able to look at you union query and understand what you're seeing.

One of my union queries is Ebook Sales By Month. It contains fields for Month, Year, Title, Identifier, Units, Revenue, and Platform. And it pulls this information in from twelve different sources.

Here is what the first part of that query looks like in SQL:

```
Ebook Sales By Month

SELECT DISTINCTROW Pronoun.Month, Pronoun.Year, [Ebook Link Table].Title, Pronoun.ISBN, Sum(Pronoun.Copies) AS
SumOfCopies, Sum(Pronoun.[Payable Earnings]) AS [SumOfPayable Earnings],'Pronoun' AS Platform
FROM [Ebook Link Table] RIGHT JOIN Pronoun ON [Ebook Link Table].[Pronoun ISBN] = Pronoun.ISBN
GROUP BY Pronoun.Month, Pronoun.Year, [Ebook Link Table].Title, Pronoun.ISBN
HAVING (((Sum(Pronoun.[Payable Earnings]))>0))

UNION

SELECT DISTINCTROW [Other Ebook].MonthOfSale, [Other Ebook].YrOfSale, [Ebook Link Table].Title, [Other Ebook].ASIN,
Sum([Other Ebook].Quantity) AS SumOfQuantity, Sum([Other Ebook].Profit) AS SumOfProfit, 'StoryBundle' AS Platform
FROM [Other Ebook] LEFT JOIN [Ebook Link Table] ON [Other Ebook].ASIN = [Ebook Link Table].ASIN
GROUP BY [Other Ebook].MonthOfSale, [Other Ebook].YrOfSale, [Ebook Link Table].Title, [Other Ebook].ASIN

UNION

SELECT DISTINCTROW Nook.Month, Nook.Year, [Ebook Link Table].Title, Nook.[BN ID / ISBN], Sum(Nook.[Net Units Sold])
AS [SumOfNet Units Sold], Sum(Nook.[Total Royalty]) AS [SumOfTotal Royalty], 'Nook' AS Platform
FROM [Ebook Link Table] RIGHT JOIN Nook ON [Ebook Link Table].Nook = Nook.[BN ID / ISBN]
WHERE (((Nook.[List Price])>0))
GROUP BY Nook.Month, Nook.Year, [Ebook Link Table].Title, Nook.[BN ID / ISBN]
HAVING (((Nook.[BN ID / ISBN]) Not Like "978*"))

UNION

SELECT DISTINCTROW [Kobo Subscriptions].Month, [Kobo Subscriptions].Year, [Ebook Link Table].Title, [Kobo
Subscriptions].eISBN, Sum([Kobo Subscriptions].Reads) AS SumOfReads, Sum([Kobo Subscriptions].[Total publisher
revenue share in payable currency ($)]) AS [SumOfTotal publisher revenue share in payable currency ($)], 'Kobo Sub' AS
Platform
FROM [Ebook Link Table] RIGHT JOIN [Kobo Subscriptions] ON [Ebook Link Table].[Kobo ID] = [Kobo Subscriptions].eISBN
GROUP BY [Kobo Subscriptions].Month, [Kobo Subscriptions].Year, [Ebook Link Table].Title, [Kobo Subscriptions].eISBN
HAVING (((Sum([Kobo Subscriptions].[Total publisher revenue share in payable currency ($)]))>0))

UNION
```

It's combining data from four different queries. (And actually because it's a copy of the SQL language in those queries, it's pulling directly from their source tables.)

Insane, right? But if you set it up right, it's a piece of cake to create. All you need is a query for each source of information that exactly matches the order of the columns you want in your union query.

For this particular query, for each of my twelve revenue sources, I wanted a query that gave me Month, Year, Title, Identifier, Units, and Revenue. That's easy enough to build. You know how to do that at this point.

So you set that up. And then you go to the Create tab and in the Queries section you click on Query Design.

(This is where you can go to build a query without using the Query Wizard should you ever want to.)

This opens a new query in Design View that has no tables or queries selected. It's a blank slate. You'll also see a Show Table dialogue box. Close that.

Now, switch over to SQL View.

You can either do that by clicking on SQL View under the Results section of the Design tab, by right-clicking into the work area and choosing SQL View from the dropdown menu, or by going to the Home tab and changing your view from there.

You will now be in SQL View with just the word SELECT visible in your workspace. Delete that.

Now open your first source query and go to SQL View for that query.

The entirety of the SQL language for that query will already be highlighted. Copy it. (Ctrl + C)

Go back to your new query workspace and paste what you copied. (Ctrl + V)

Delete the semi-colon from the end of what you just pasted.

Hit Enter twice. (You really don't have to do this but I find it's visually cleaner if I do.)

Type UNION

Open your second source query and copy that over to your new query the same way you did with the first source query.

If you have a third query to add then delete the semi-colon, hit Enter a couple times, type UNION, and copy the next source into your query. Keep going until all of your sources have been added.

If not, you're done.

As long as you built your queries to have identical columns, to only include the columns/fields you wanted in your union query, and to have the same data types, then you should be done at this point.

Change your view to Datasheet View and you should see the information from your source queries all combined into one table nice and neat.

If your source queries don't match up, then you're going to need to edit what you pasted in until they do.

Here is an example where I've pasted in two queries that I want to include in my union query:

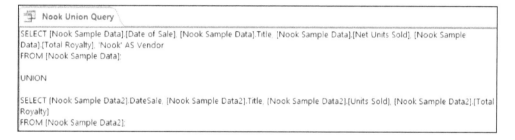

But it isn't working. When I try to look at it in Datasheet View I get an error message telling me that the number of columns in the two selected queries doesn't match. Which is correct. Because if you look closely at the first listed query, there's an additional field/column in that query called Vendor that isn't in the second one.

At this point I can either add a Vendor column to the second table. It's a fixed value so I'd just add a comma and then whatever I wanted that query's fixed value to be in single quotes and then AS Vendor. Or I can delete that text from the first query description.

I chose to add to the second query. Now I have this:

```
Nook Union Query

SELECT [Nook Sample Data].[Date of Sale], [Nook Sample Data].Title, [Nook Sample Data].[Net Units Sold], [Nook Sample
Data].[Total Royalty], 'Nook' AS Vendor
FROM [Nook Sample Data];

UNION

SELECT [Nook Sample Data2].DateSale, [Nook Sample Data2].Title, [Nook Sample Data2].[Units Sold], [Nook Sample Data2].[Total
Royalty], 'Nook2' AS Vendor
FROM [Nook Sample Data2];
```

And when I switch to Datasheet View it looks like this:

| Date of Sale ▾ | Title ▾ | Net Units Sol ▾ | Total Royalty ▾ | Vendor ▾ |
|---|---|---|---|---|
| | | | | Nook |
| 8/1/2017 | A Title | 1 | 0.12345656 | Nook |
| 8/1/2017 | A Title | 1 | 1.25 | Nook2 |
| 8/1/2017 | A Title | 1 | 2.6 | Nook2 |
| 8/2/2017 | A Title | 1 | 0 | Nook |
| 8/2/2017 | A Title | 1 | 3.21 | Nook2 |
| 8/2/2017 | Another Title | 1 | 2.56 | Nook2 |
| 8/3/2017 | A Third Title | 1 | 3.56 | Nook2 |
| 8/3/2017 | A Title | 1 | 0 | Nook |
| 8/3/2017 | A Title | 1 | 1.48 | Nook2 |
| 8/6/2017 | A Title | 1 | 0 | Nook |

This query happens to have sorted on date so the results from the two source queries are blended together but you can see in the far-right column which query contributed which record.

It's that simple as long as your base queries were set up the right way.

Just remember if you do add a fixed field like that to do so within the SELECT clause portion of your SQL statement and not after one of the other clauses.

Also, make sure that you have the same number of fields in each of the source queries you use and that they match up in terms of order and content. And that you include UNION between each one.

* * *

A few more things to know about union queries.

They are listed at the bottom of your queries and sorted separately from your select queries. You can identify a union query because it is shown with two interlocking circles on the left-hand side of the name as opposed to the two stacked data tables shown for select queries.

There is no Design View for a union query. You can only open it in Datasheet View or in SQL View.

Also, and this may just happen with Access 2013, but I've never been able to get a union query to keep a summation if I add it to the bottom of the query by using Totals in the Records section of the Home tab. I can add totals while working in the query and see the values at the bottom, but when I close and reopen the query that summation is gone. Just click on Totals again and they'll reappear so you don't have to recreate them from scratch.

(On their website Microsoft provides a workaround for how to add a summary line to your union query but it's pretty ugly and I'm not inclined to use it.)

If you're comfortable enough in Access you can add at the end of your SQL statement an ORDER BY clause to set the sort order for your query. I generally just do this in Datasheet View and save when I close.

In the past I've had issues with my union queries when I forgot to delete the semi-colon after each of my pasted-in queries (except for the last one), but I wasn't able to replicate that just now. I'd recommend though that as a best practice you only have a semi-colon at the very end of your SQL statement.

Access will take the field names for your query from the field names used in the first query you pasted in. So if you want to control the field names, do so in that source query.

If you're pasting in an entire table, you can use

SELECT * from [Table Name]

instead of pasting in the individual selected field names.

Also, as mentioned in *Access for Beginners*, when I changed my field names using the Field Name: Field Name Description format, it broke a couple of my union queries. But not all of them. I believe that the ones where I had copied and pasted the entire SQL text from an existing query updated correctly, but the ones where I'd cleaned up that SQL text or typed it in myself were the ones that broke.

When those broke I knew it had happened because I saw an Enter Parameters dialogue box appear when I tried to open the union query the next time.

Also, I talked in this entire section about using queries to generate your union query. Technically, you can use tables as well. You just need to know how to create the SQL statement to do that. Since I think it's easier to create a query first and then just copy and paste that over, I didn't cover it here. But you can see in the screenshot above with the four pasted in queries exactly how you could write that. Each of those pasted in portions are in fact pulling data directly from two source tables.

# QUERIES:
# CROSSTAB QUERIES

Another type of query that I sometimes use is called a crosstab query. (I often just dump my query results into Excel and use a Pivot Table instead.) The nice thing about crosstab queries as opposed to the dumping into Excel method is that you only have to create them that one time.

Basically what a crosstab query does is it puts one set of values across the top of the table, another across the left-hand side, and at the intersection of those two values it shows you the designated result for the two variable you're combining.

For example, I have a crosstab query for Words Published Per Author Per Year. Here it is:

| Author Name | 2013 | 2014 | 2015 | 2016 | 2017 | 2018 | 2019 | 2020 | Total Words |
|---|---|---|---|---|---|---|---|---|---|
| Author1 | | | | | | 46,204 | 141,177 | 42,221 | 229,602 |
| Author2 | | | 109,000 | 93,305 | 84,955 | | | | 287,260 |
| Author3 | | | 54,364 | 17,077 | 5,982 | | | | 77,423 |
| Author4 | | 71,620 | | 44,448 | 86,949 | | | | 203,017 |
| Author5 | | 9,551 | 19,928 | | | | | | 29,479 |
| Author6 | | 46,262 | 65,365 | 7,998 | 25,606 | | | | 145,231 |
| Author7 | 27,278 | 53,614 | 32,441 | 30,142 | 20,397 | | | | 163,872 |
| Author8 | 27,121 | 17,960 | 14,639 | 90,281 | | | | | 150,001 |
| Author9 | | | 69,330 | | 162,964 | 155,412 | 210,290 | 14,604 | 612,600 |
| Total | 54,399 | 199,007 | 365,067 | 283,251 | 386,853 | 201,616 | 351,467 | 56,825 | 1,898,485 |

I have Year across the top. Author Name on the left-hand side. And at the intersection of those two I have the total wordcount for each combination.

You can name a query anything you want, but I tend to name them with what I'm calculating and then the two variables I'm looking at for that calculation.

You can see here that you can also include a grand total column for each row. This is done as part of building the query.

And a total for each column. This is done using the Totals option in the Records section of the Home tab.

\* \* \*

Okay. So let's create one of these.

I use the Query Wizard for this which means that I need a single table or query that has all of my information in it. (If you're very comfortable in Access you can create a crosstab query that uses more than one table or query, but we're not going to cover that here, because you can't use the Query Wizard to do that.)

First step. Choose the Query Wizard from the Queries section of the Create tab. (You don't have to click on the table or query you want to use at this point because it will ignore you anyway.)

In the first screen of the Query Wizard choose Crosstab Query Wizard and click OK.

This will bring up the Crosstab Query Wizard dialogue box where you need to choose the table or query you want to use.

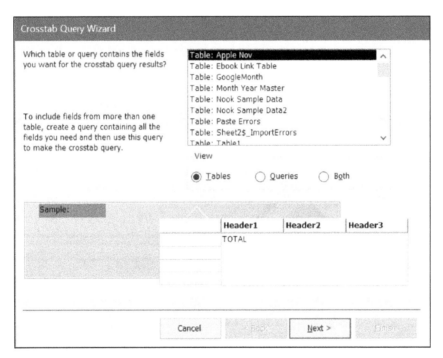

Note that by default it shows your tables, but you can change that by clicking on the circle next to Queries or the circle next to Both right below the table listing.

Choose the table or query you want to use and then click Next.

Now it's time to choose your row headings. This is the variable you want along the *side* of your crosstab query result. (For some reason the way they phrase this question I always think it's my column headers but it's not.)

When you choose a field it will display in the preview screen at the bottom of the dialogue box, like so, where I've chosen Title for my row headings:

You can select up to three fields for your row headings, just keep in mind that if the three fields are not exclusively related to one another (like title, author, series generally would be where each title only has one associated series name and one author) that this will increase the number of rows in your table because there will be a row for each combination of your three selected row heading fields.

After you've selected your row headings, click Next.

Now you can select your columns heading field. The preview down below will show whichever field you're currently clicked onto as the header field. Note that it doesn't label the column with that name. What displays in the column headers are the values for that selected field.

Choose your field and click Next.

I chose a date field so my next option is the time interval I want to use for my dates. I can choose Year, Quarter, Month, Date, or Date/Time.

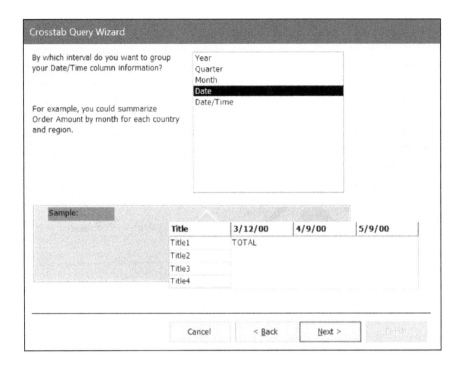

The preview does not show actual dates from your data. It just shows generic examples of what those column headers will look like under each option. If you have a date field, make your selection, and click Next.

If you chose a numeric or text field instead of a date field, Access will go straight to the screen which asks what number you want calculated in the table.

In the fields selection box choose the field whose values you want calculated in the center of the table and then in the functions selection box choose what calculation you want.

In this case I'm going to click on Total Royalty and Sum to have the query calculate the sum of total royalties for each title for each day. You can see that's what I'm going to get in the preview section where it says Sum(Total Royalty):

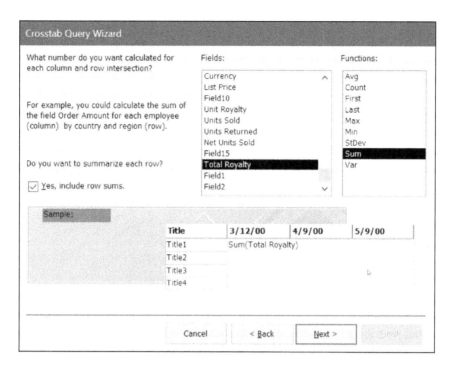

Also, this is where you can tell Access if you want a column added to your table that shows the total value for each row. I tend to leave that checked because I do want to see the total for each row, but if you don't care about that you can uncheck it.

Click Next.

Change your query name if you want. If you don't it will be your source file name with Query_Crosstab added at the end.

I always choose to view the query, but if you are comfortable enough in Access that this was just a base for you to work from, then you might choose modify the design to see the query in Design View instead.

Click Finish.

And here you go:

That was created from this data:

| Nook Sample Data2_Crosstab | | Nook Sample Data2 | |
|---|---|---|---|
| DateSale ▾ | Title ▾ | Units Sold ▾ | Total Royalty ▾ |
| 8/1/2017 | A Title | 1 | 1.25 |
| 8/2/2017 | Another Title | 1 | 2.56 |
| 8/3/2017 | A Third Title | 1 | 3.56 |
| 8/10/2017 | A Third Title | 1 | 4.21 |
| 8/6/2017 | Check | 1 | 3.14 |
| 8/10/2017 | Check | 1 | 1.87 |
| 8/10/2017 | A Title | 2 | 1.21 |
| 1/1/2019 | A Title | 1 | 0.93 |
| 8/1/2017 | A Title | 1 | 2.6 |
| 8/2/2017 | A Title | 1 | 3.21 |
| 8/3/2017 | A Title | 1 | 1.48 |
| 8/6/2017 | A Title | 1 | 5.1 |
| 8/10/2017 | A Title | 1 | 1.2 |

A few things to note here.

The summary column for each row is the *second* column instead of showing at the end of the table. It's easy enough to left-click on the column and drag it to the end, which is what I always do with these queries. But because Access by default wants to put that summary column on the left-hand side, I find that when new columns of data are added to a crosstab query I have to move the summary column again or it ends up stuck in the middle between the entries that were already in the table and the new ones. (So, for example, in this query if my source data had a new date added, this would happen.)

At this point there is also not a summary row for each column. To add one, use the Totals option in the Records section of the Home tab and then go through for each column and select Sum in the Total row. When you save, close, and later reopen the crosstab query that totals row will not be visible. But if you click once more on Totals in the Records section of the Home tab it will reappear.

One final adjustment I make to my crosstab queries is to rename that totals column. Right now mine is showing Total of Tota… and the rest of the label is hidden. To rename that column in a crosstab query, go to the Design View for the table, click on the entry that says Total of Tota… and change the *Caption* for that column in the Property Sheet.

While I was in Design View I also changed the format for the royalties fields in the Property Sheet to Currency with 2 decimal places. I had to change the formatting for the summary column separately.

All of those changes gave me this:

| Nook Sample Data2_Crosstab | | | | | | | |
|---|---|---|---|---|---|---|---|
| Title ▾ | 1/1/2019 ▾ | 8/1/2017 ▾ | 8/10/2017 ▾ | 8/2/2017 ▾ | 8/3/2017 ▾ | 8/6/2017 ▾ | Total Royalty ▾ |
| A Third Title | | | $4.21 | | $3.56 | | $7.77 |
| A Title | $0.93 | $3.85 | $2.41 | $3.21 | $1.48 | $5.10 | $16.98 |
| Another Title | | | | $2.56 | | | $2.56 |
| Check | | | $1.87 | | | $3.14 | $5.01 |
| Total | $0.93 | $3.85 | $8.49 | $5.77 | $5.04 | $8.24 | $32.32 |

And there we go. A simple crosstab query of Total Royalty by Title and by Date.

A crosstab query can be edited in Design View and/or SQL View.

* * *

One final note. Your crosstab queries will be listed in their own section above your select queries and will show with an image next to them of a single data table with a darker first row and a darker first column.

So in this image we have one crosstab query, five select queries, and one union query.

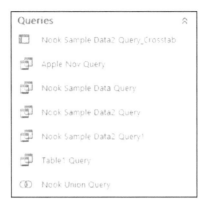

# QUERIES:
## ASKING FOR USER INPUT IN A QUERY

Another type of query that you may want to use is a parameter query that asks users to provide input values that are then used as calculations in your query.

I've never had to use this one but I can see where it might come in handy if you've written a query that includes a calculation but there is a part of that calculation that can vary.

Say, for example, that I have a query that lists a series of loans I've made where I'm expecting payment. And that I want to discount the value of those loans by a certain percentage based upon how many people I expect to default on their payments. But that that percentage varies over time. When the economy is good, most people pay what they owe. When it's bad, though, a lot more people stop paying.

In that case, I can set up my query so that every time I run it, it asks me to provide the discount rate. It's far better to do that than run the query with a fixed discount rate baked into an equation in the query and have to remember to change it. (Also, that goes against good data principles where you show your assumptions.)

* * *

So. To create a parameter query that will ask a user for a value, open your query in Design View.

If it's important that the query or your ultimate report contain your assumed value (and I'd argue that's generally the case), then create a new field for that value with whatever name you want to assign it and a description of what it needs in brackets.

For example, if I want to have a field named Payout Percent, then I might write:

Payout Percent: [Enter Payout Percent]

for my new field in Design View.

That would give me a column labeled Payout Percent and every single time I opened that query I would see an Enter Parameter Value dialogue box that said "Enter Payout Percent".

The one thing here that you can't have is Payout Percent: [Payout Percent] because it will create a

49

circular reference and refuse to run. So your field name has to be different from whatever you put in brackets for the dialogue box to display.

Also, don't make your text in the brackets the same as any of your field names or else Access will just treat it like a reference to that field.

If you do it this way, you can then also have a calculation in the query that uses the value provided in that field.

Here I've created the field Payout Percent and then used it in a calculation that combines it with my field Proceeds:

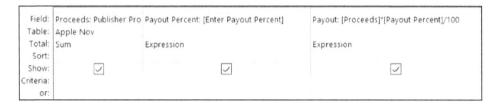

When I then run the query in Datasheet View Access will show a parameter dialogue box with the text Enter Payout Percent, will populate the value I give it into the Payout Percent column and will then use that value I provided for the calculations in the Payout column.

Here is an example where I provided the value of 20:

| Proceeds | Payout Percent | Payout |
|---|---|---|
|  |  | 20 |
| 2.8 | 20 | 0.56 |
| 10.49 | 20 | 2.098 |
| 7.45 | 20 | 1.49 |
| 4.16 | 20 | 0.832 |
| 5.6 | 20 | 1.12 |

\* \* \*

You don't have to give your new input variable its own field. You can just create the calculation and have it ask for the value. But if you do that then be sure to use the bracketed portion of your new input so that users know what to provide.

So instead of using:

Payout: [Proceeds]*[Payout Percent]/100

like I did for the formula above. I would use:

Payout: [Proceeds]*[Enter Payout Percent]/100

instead.

This would give me the same result, but it would make sure that the parameter dialogue box that the user saw said "Enter Payout Percent".

(And looking at this and how it works I'd probably change that to [Enter Payout Percent as a Whole Number] or something like that to make it clear that I didn't want them to enter .2 or 20% for the value.)

\* \* \*

So there you have it. Basically treat the text you want the user to see for your Enter Parameter Value dialogue box as a named field with brackets around it wherever you want to collect that information. And if you do so in a separate field then you can name that field and use that name in any other expressions you write that use it.

# QUERIES:
# A BRIEF MENTION OF OTHER QUERY TYPES

As I've mentioned previously, I use Access as an Excel user who needs more capability than Excel can give me. I do not use it as a computer programmer or database developer. This means that I use it more for analysis than I do as a standalone database. Which means that there are additional query types that I don't use because they're more the types of queries someone would use for maintaining a database.

But I wanted to mention them briefly in case you ever need one so that you know they exist and what to call them. All of the queries below are very powerful and have the ability to significantly transform your database so use them with caution and definitely backup your database first. You can wipe out data with the click of a button with some of these queries and you won't be able to get it back. So proceed with caution and be sure it's what you want to do before you act.

Having said that, your additional available queries are:

## Append Query

Append queries allow you to update a table in your database using other records in that same database. So, as I mentioned before, I used to use Append queries to update a table of total sales by month before I figured out how to use a union query to get that information instead.

The way to create an append query is to create a basic select query and then transform it into an append query where you map the fields in the query to the table where you want to append your results. So Title to Title, Author to Author, etc.

You *run* an append query as opposed to opening it to view results in a data table.

## Make-Table Query

I have never used a make-table query, but according to Access this is a query you would use to merge two existing tables of data or to make a new table out of a query. One advantage here is that the new table can be in a different database.

Be careful here, because when you create the new table it is now standalone and no longer connected to its source data. You basically create a select query, convert it to a make-table query, tell Access where to put the new table, and then run it.

## Update Query

You can use an update query to update the value of a specific field in a table. It's a bit like using the Find and Replace function but amped up a lot more. It can only be used on existing records, not to add or delete a record.

Be very careful when using an update query since it is possible to update records in more than one table at a time.

## Find Duplicate Records Query

There is a Query Wizard for this one. You tell it which tables and which fields in those tables you want to compare. This is a good query to use with a multi-user database where more than one person may have entered the same information.

## Delete Records Query

You basically create a query that contains the records you want to delete and then in Design View change the query over to a delete query from a select query and run it.

But be very, very careful here because if you didn't actually use any criteria to narrow down your results then you'll delete all of the content in your table with one little click.

# FORMS: AN OVERVIEW

The type of form we're going to cover here is what's referred to as a bound form because it ties back to a table or query with data in it that can be viewed and/or amended via the use of the form interface in Access.

As I mentioned in *Access for Beginners* a form can be a user-friendly way to present the information in a table. Rather than force someone to view the information in a grid of columns and rows you can present that same information in a one page per record format that is organized for ease of use.

For all of the forms we're going to discuss below, it won't actually be saved in your database until you choose to save it or choose to close and save it. That will also be when you have the opportunity to name the form.

# Basic Form

For lack of a better term, the "basic" form option provides all the information related to one record on a single page. You create a basic form in Access by clicking on your source table or query, going to the Forms section of the Create tab, and clicking on Form.

You will then see a page in the main workspace that contains all of the fields from the source object with values pulled from the first record in that source.

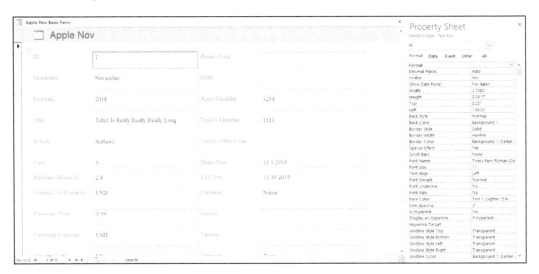

There should also be a property sheet pane on the right-hand side. At the bottom of the workspace you can navigate to each page to see the values for each record are using the arrows.

## Split Form

A split form lets you see both a form version of the data and a datasheet version of the data at the same time. The two views are linked and you can edit the entries in either the form or the datasheet. Using a split form can help you locate a specific record in less time than if you had to search or page through one record at a time.

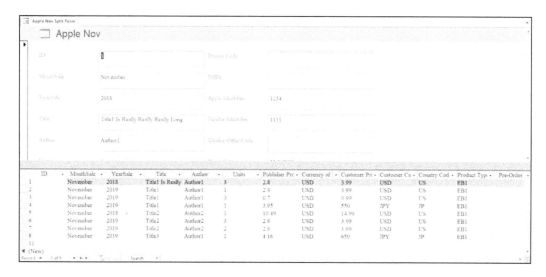

To create a split form, select your table or query, go to the Forms section of the Create tab, and select Split Form from the More Forms dropdown menu.

Once you do so you will see a basic form like before, but it will only take up a portion of the workspace. Below that will be the source data in datasheet view. Clicking into a cell in the datasheet view will immediately change the data that is displayed in the form portion of the view to match that record and will also select the corresponding cell for that record.

The arrows at the bottom of the workspace can still be used to page through the records like in the basic form view. You will also have the property sheet pane visible when the form is first created.

## Multiple Items Form

You can also create a multiple items form which will display more than one record per page. Even though this option looks a lot like the datasheet view it gives you more control over which field to include in the form (making it more user-friendly for input or review) and also more control over formatting.

To create a multiple items form, click on the table or query you want to use, go to the Forms section of the Create tab, click on the dropdown under More Forms, and choose Multiple Items. You'll basically get a grid of rows and columns just like exist in your source query or table.

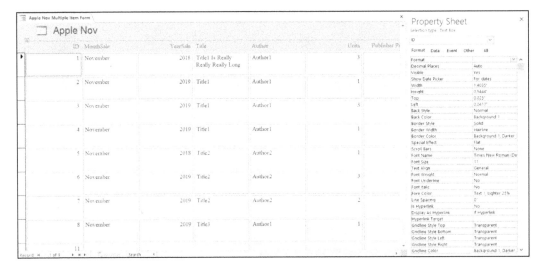

Using the arrows at the bottom will move one record at a time.

## Datasheet Form

The datasheet form option just basically looks like your datasheet except it's a form so you have control over formatting. To create it, click on your source table or query, go to the Forms section under the Create tab, and choose Datasheet from the More Forms dropdown menu.

| ID | MonthSale | YearSale | Title | Author | Units | Publisher Prc | Currency of ] | Customer Pri | Customer Cu |
|---|---|---|---|---|---|---|---|---|---|
| 1 | November | 2018 | Title1 Is Really | Author1 | 3 | 2.8 | USD | 3.99 | USD |
| 2 | November | 2019 | Title1 | Author1 | 1 | 2.8 | USD | 3.99 | USD |
| 3 | November | 2019 | Title1 | Author1 | 3 | 0.7 | USD | 0.99 | USD |
| 4 | November | 2019 | Title1 | Author1 | 1 | 3.95 | USD | 550 | JPY |
| 5 | November | 2018 | Title2 | Author2 | 1 | 10.49 | USD | 14.99 | USD |
| 6 | November | 2019 | Title2 | Author2 | 3 | 2.8 | USD | 3.99 | USD |
| 7 | November | 2019 | Title2 | Author2 | 2 | 2.8 | USD | 3.99 | USD |
| 8 | November | 2019 | Title3 | Author1 | 1 | 4.16 | USD | 650 | JPY |
| 11 | | | | | | | | | |
| * (New) | | | | | | | | | |

# REPORTS: AN OVERVIEW

A report lets you create a nice, summarized printable document that displays your information in a user-friendly way. It can have custom headers, footers, and field labels. You can determine font size and adding bolding, italics, change the colors, etc. And it can have summary statistics at various levels. (I have reports that provide detail information by title but also summarize values at the author and series level as well.)

There are two primary ways to create a report, the Report Tool and the Report Wizard.

## Report Tool

The Report Tool is very simple to use. It will take whatever table or query you're using as the source document and create a report from it that includes all of your fields. To use it, click on the table or query you want to use, go to the Create tab, and click on Report in the Reports section.

You will immediately see a basic report, like this one:

I usually find that I need to refine any report that Access creates for me using the Report Tool, because, as you can see with this one, the fields run off the page to a second page so the report is not immediately printable.

A report generated this way will open in Layout View which is a view where you can edit the report while still seeing what it will look like on the page. (We'll talk about form and report views more in a minute.)

## Report Wizard

Your other option is to use the Report Wizard. This allows you to choose fields from more than one table or query to build your report. (I'll confess here that I'm more comfortable creating a query that combines all of the values I want to use and building a report from there, but that's probably just my own nervousness at play.)

Click on the first table or query you want to use, go to the Create tab, and click on Report Wizard in the Reports section. This will bring up the Report Wizard dialogue box:

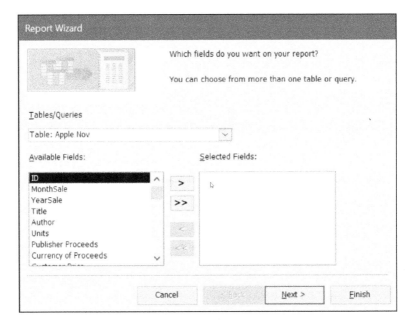

Just like with the *query* wizard, you can then choose the fields you want to use. And just like with the query wizard, if you choose fields from more than one source you need to have relationships established between those tables and queries beforehand.

Click Next when you're done choosing your fields.

You'll then be asked if you want to group your data on any of your selected fields.

Grouping your data, which we'll discuss more later, essentially displays it by the values for that field. So if I group on year, then my data will be listed based on the year with details underneath each year heading.

Here I've chosen to group on year of sale. Note how that field is now shown as a label above the other fields:

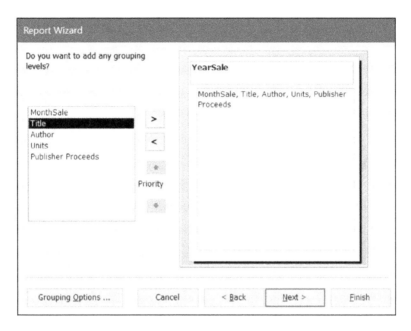

If you click on the Grouping Options button after you've selected at least one field to group by, you can then choose to group text based on X number of letters or your numeric values based on the 10s, 100s, etc. (I don't really use either one.)

If you group on more than one field, you can use the arrows to prioritize which field is used first.

When you're done choosing the fields to group by, click Next.

This screen lets you choose how to sort your data and how to summarize your data.

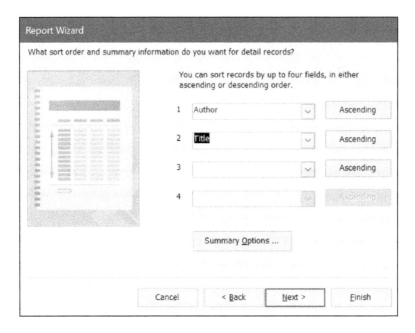

Here I've chosen to sort by Author and then by Title in ascending order.

Clicking on the Summary Options button allows you to tell Access if you want to take the sum, average, min, or max of any of your numeric values. You can choose to do so and only display the summary values or to do so and display both the detail and summary values on the right-hand side.

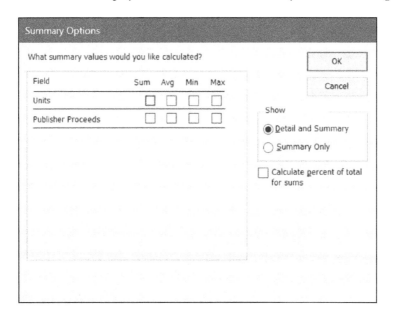

You can also choose to calculate the percent of the total for your summed values on the right-hand side as well. (I generally don't do so.)

Click OK to close Summary Options and Next to move to the next screen where you have the choice between a Stepped, Block, or Outline layout for your report. Clicking on each option will give you a generic preview of that option on the left-hand side of the dialogue box.

You can also choose here to adjust the field width so that all of the fields fit onto the page and choose a Portrait or Landscape orientation. If you have many columns of data, choosing the Landscape orientation will help the data better fit on the page.

When you're done, click Next. Change your report name if you want. Click Finish.

Here's our sample report:

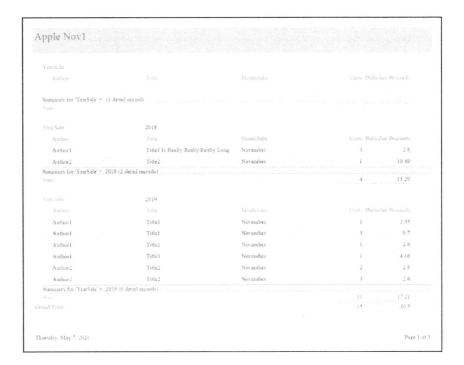

Here's the data that was used to generate it:

## Other Options

In addition to Report and Report Wizard you also have Report Design which opens a blank report in Design View and lets you build your report completely from scratch, and Blank Report which does the same thing but in Layout View. There could be a time when you'd want to work that way, but you're probably far better off using the Report Wizard or starting with a basic report and going from there.

The reports section also lets you create labels, but as I've said before I think there are far better off-the-shelf commercial solutions for customer contact databases these days so I'll just mention that that capability exists but I'm not going to cover it.

# FORMS AND REPORTS:
# VIEWS

We're about to talk about how to work with an existing form or report to customize it and since it's pretty much the same for both of them I'm going to cover a lot of this material together. But first I want to walk through the view options you have available to you.

As a reminder, you can always change your view in the Home tab using the View dropdown. However, with Forms and Reports, you can also right-click in the unused space in a form or report and choose your view from the dropdown menu that way. Also, in Layout View and Design View there is a View dropdown in the Design tab.

## Form View

This is the default view when you open an existing form and is what your finished product looks like. It has all of your data showing.

You can navigate to each record using the arrows at the bottom or by inputting the record number you want. If the data on a specific page is more than you can see in the workspace there will also be scroll bars you can use.

In Form View, you can change values if the form was based upon a table or a basic query with fields that tied directly back to a table. You can't change summary values.

You can move between cells in a form using the arrow keys or Tab and Shift + Tab.

## Report View

This is the default view when you open an existing report. It too shows all of your final data.

In the Report View it's all one large page. You can use the scroll bars on the right-hand side to scroll upward and downward, or on the bottom of the workspace to scroll to the left or the right.

Values in a report cannot be edited, but you can click into a cell and use the Tab and Shift + Tab keys to move between values. (Although I've never seen a need to do so.)

# Print Preview

Print Preview is available as a view option for reports, but not for forms. If you select this view it will show you the report one printable page at a time. This is the view that lets you see if any of your columns run onto a second page or if any of your groups break in a way that you don't like.

When in print preview you can navigate between the printable pages using the arrows or input box at the bottom of the workspace. Use the scroll bars to see the parts of the page that aren't currently visible in the workspace.

You may not actually be able to see the entire page by default because of the zoom level of your workspace. To change the zoom level, you can use the slider in the bottom right corner of the screen. Just click and drag the white bar to the left until the full page is visible in your workspace. Keep in mind that doing so may make the document too small for you to read the text, but it does give a better idea of the visual presentation of your data than using the scroll bars does.

To return to Report View, click on Close Print Preview under the Close Preview section of the Print Preview tab.

I should also note here that while forms don't have a view option of Print Preview you can still choose to Print from the File tab and then choose Print Preview there if you want to see how a form will print.

# Layout View

The Form View, Report View, and Print Preview all just let you look at the form or report in question, but they don't let you edit it. That can only be done in the Layout View and the Design View.

Layout View keeps the form or report looking mostly the same as it will when it prints, except now you have the ability to make edits to your form or report. You can right-click on a column and see all sorts of available options or you can use the Layout Tools tabs up top for that form or report to change the design, arrangement, format, or, for reports, page setup.

Here is a report in layout view:

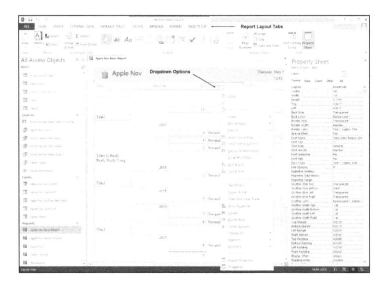

You can see up top that there is a Report Layout Tools header with four tabs under it, Design, Arrange, Format, and Page Setup. I've also right-clicked on the MonthSale column and you can see that there is a large dropdown menu with a number of available choices. On the right-hand side there is also the Property Sheet for the MonthSale field which provides the current formatting for that field, all of which can be edited from there as well.

## Design View

Design View is very similar to Layout View except you don't see your data. It's working with the underlying template instead. I suspect most people would prefer to work in Layout View. For some reason I usually work in Design View.

Design View also has a Design Tools header with Design, Arrange, and Format tabs below that, as well as for reports, Page Setup. There are also options listed when you right-click a field. And there is a Property Sheet for each field that lets you see how it's currently formatted and amend that formatting.

Here is the Design View for the report shown above in Layout View with a dropdown menu and the property sheet shown:

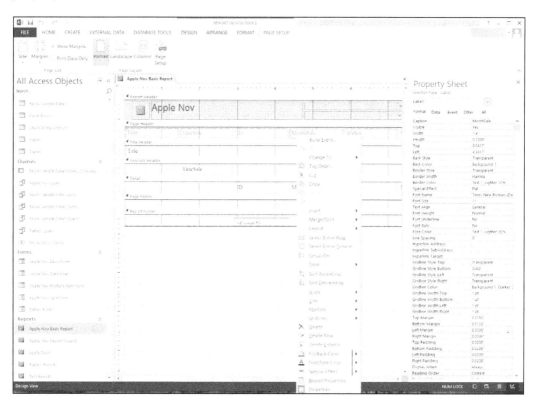

I think the nice thing about Design View is that I can work on an entire report, no matter how many pages long it is, and it's generally all there on the screen for me. For example, here is a screenshot of Design View for an eight-page report.

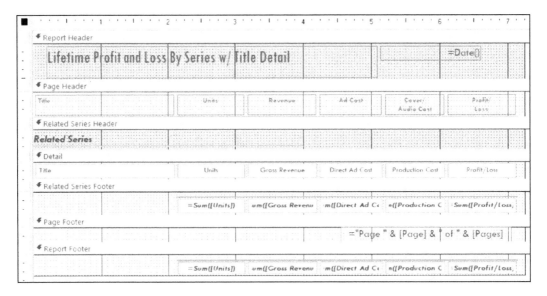

In Layout View I'd have to work with this report across all eight pages, but in Design View it's compacted down to just this small space. The problem with working in Design View though is that it's harder to tell when an entry doesn't fit or columns go off the edge of the page. So when I do work in Design View I have to frequently switch to Form or Report View to make sure that what I've done works in that view as well.

# FORMS AND REPORTS:
## EDITING AND FORMATTING TEXT BOXES

As discussed above, if you want to edit a form or report you need to do so either in Layout View or Design View. There are usually at least two ways to change formatting, one involving the Property Sheet and one involving the Design, Arrange, and Format tabs at the top of the screen.

I tend to use the Property Sheet because it's all right there in one spot, but the tabs are probably the more user-friendly option.

When you switch to either Layout or Design View the Property Sheet should be visible on the right-hand side of the screen. Here's what it looks like:

If it isn't, you can go to the Design tab and click on Property Sheet in the Tools section. Or you can right-click on the workspace for the form or report and choose Properties from the dropdown menu.

\* \* \*

If you open a form or report in Layout or Design View you will notice that the Design, Arrange, and Format tabs I mentioned above are actually shown under a header section. Depending on which you opened and which view you chose that could be Form Layout Tools, Report Layout Tools, Form Design Tools, or Report Design Tools.

Normally in telling you where to go to perform a task I would reference those header sections, but I'm not going to here because regardless of which one you're in the steps I'm going to discuss remain the same and the tab names remain the same.

So I'll just be referring to the Design, Arrange, and Format tabs which will be displayed under a header that I'm not going to reference.

\* \* \*

Another note before we begin, Ctrl + Z to Undo does seem to work when formatting forms or reports and does work for more than one formatting change at a time, so if you mess up simply Ctrl + Z to Undo until you're back to what you had before and then try again.

\* \* \*

Also, Access distinguishes between labels and text boxes. Labels contain fixed values and are usually associated with a text box that displays the actual data for a record. Think of labels as your column headers in a data table or query and text boxes as your values for each record from that table or query. They look a lot alike and can generally be edited in the same way, so from here on out I'm going to refer to them generically as text boxes unless what I say only applies to one or the other.

\* \* \*

And, finally, for all of the options below you need to click on the text box you want to edit before you make your edit. I'll explicitly state that for the first few so you get the hang of it, but then I'm just going to assume that you know to do so.

\* \* \*

## Resize a Text Box

To change the size of a text box you have a few options.

You can click on the box you want to change and then move your cursor until it's along the edge of the box and you see a two-sided arrow either pointing to the left and right or up and down. You can then left-click and drag the box to the desired size at that point.

Usually this will change the width of all text boxes in a column or the height of all text boxes in a row, not just the one you chose to resize. If all the text boxes don't change at once and you wanted them to, you can select multiple text boxes by using the Ctrl key as you click on each one, and then when you click and drag on one text box it will resize them all.

(For Reports, you can't change the row height of your data text boxes in Layout View with this option, but you can change the row height of the text boxes in your header section. You need to go to Design View for your data text boxes or use the option we'll discuss next.)

Your other option for resizing a text box is to click into the box you want to change and in the Property Sheet on the right-hand side of the screen change the values for Width and/or Height. (About the fourth or fifth ones down.)

This too will most likely change the width and height for the entire column or row. (And it works on any cell you click in, including the data input fields for a Report in Layout View.)

## Remove the Border Around a Text Box

If you don't want a visible border around a text box in your form or report, you can:

Select the box or boxes you want to modify, go to the Control Formatting section of the Format tab, click on the Shape Outline dropdown arrow, and choose Transparent.

You can also click on the dropdown arrow under Shape Outline, go to the Line Type option at the bottom, and chose the blank line choice which is at the very top of the Line Type dropdown.

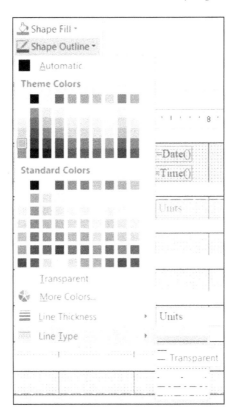

Note that this will work with Design View as well as Layout View but that you won't be able to see that the format change is in effect in the workspace in Design View. The box will still look like it has borders around it. However, your change will be reflected in the Property Sheet and you will be able to see it if you switch to Form or Report View.

Your other option to remove the visible border from around a box is to use the Property Sheet. The option you want to change there is called Border Style and is about eleven rows down.

After you click into the cell related to Border Style you will be able to choose between Transparent, Solid, Dashes, Short Dashes, Dot, Sparse Dots, Dash Dot, or Dash Dot Dot. Choosing transparent will remove the line.

## Add a Border Around a Text Box

To add a border around a box, you have the same options you had for removing the border.

You can use the Shape Outline dropdown in the Format tab to choose your line type. (For a simple border it's the single line which is the second option in the Line Type dropdown.)

Or you can use the Property Sheet to change the Border Style.

## Change the Color or Thickness of the Border Around a Text Box

If you want to change the color of the line around a text box, go to the Shape Outline dropdown in the Format tab, and choose a different color.

Or you can change the selection in the Border Color dropdown in the Property Sheet. To see the same color options that you have in the Format tab, click on the … next to the dropdown arrow for Border Color.

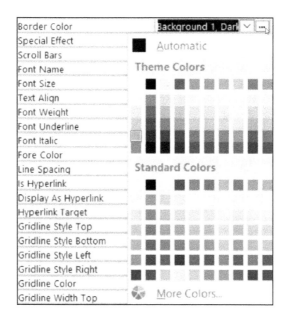

If you want to change the width of the line used for the border, this can be done in the Shape Outline dropdown by choosing a different option for Line Thickness. In the Property Sheet the change can be made under Border Width.

## Adding Grid Lines Around Text Boxes

In addition to the basic line you can add around a text box, you can also add what Access calls a gridline. These are separate from your Border Style.

In the image below there are three text boxes with borders around them, but only the bottom text box has a gridline above it. The gridline is associated with the text box, but separate from the lines used to provide a border around it.

| 8 | November |
|---|----------|
| 9 | |

I always add gridlines using the Property Sheet, so we'll cover that option first, but you can also do so through the Arrange tab.

In the Property Sheet there are four rows that let you add gridlines called Gridline Style Top, Gridline Style Bottom, Gridline Style Left, and Gridline Style Right. And then below that are rows for Gridline Color and for determining the width of each of the four types of gridline.

(You can find these options towards the bottom of the visible property sheet choices if you're using the default zoom level. If not, it's about 27 rows down where the first gridline option starts.)

The gridline style choices are the same as for a border, Transparent, Solid, Dashes, Short Dashes, etc. But the line you add can be a single line on the top, bottom, or either side of a text box. For this reason, gridlines are a good choice for separating out summary values, like in the example above. You put a thick grid line above the text box that contains the summary value to distinguish it from the values it's summing up.

You can change the color of the gridline using the Gridline Color box and you can make the line thicker using the Gridline Width box for each gridline. The example above used a 2 pt gridline.

Often when you're adding sums into a report Access will include gridlines for you by default.

To add, edit, or remove a gridline, click onto the related text box, and then make your choices in the appropriate rows in the Property Sheet. To remove an existing gridline change the Gridline Style to Transparent.

Your other option for gridlines is to go to the Table section of the Arrange tab where it says Gridlines. Click on the dropdown arrow under Gridlines to see your available choices.

Choosing Both will put four gridlines around your text box. Horizontal will put a top and bottom gridline. Vertical will put a left and right gridline. Top will put one on top of the text box. Bottom will put one on the bottom of the text box. None will remove any existing gridlines.

When you make a new choice, it overrides your old choice, so if you want a strange gridline combination like one side and the bottom you'd have to do that in the Property Sheet.

You can also change the color, line width, and line style using the Color, Width, and Border options in the dropdown. These changes can be made either before you insert your gridline or after you insert it.

## Change the Background Color of a Text Box

To fill a label or text box with a color, you can go to the Format tab, choose Shape Fill, and select your color from there.

Or you can change the Back Color option in the Property Sheet. (About the tenth option listed.)

If you use the Property sheet click on the ... to see all available colors.

When you make this change it will be immediately visible in both Layout View and Design View.

If you need to revert back to the original settings, the default background color for the base theme is Background 1 in the Property Sheet or Automatic in the Shape Fill dropdown.

## Change the Font Color in a Text Box

To change the color of the text in a label or text box, you can either go to the Text Formatting section of the Home tab or the Font section of the Format tab, and click on the dropdown arrow next to the A, and choose your font color from there.

(Automatic will return the font color to the default color.)

Or you can use the Property Sheet and change the value for Fore Color (which is located a little more than halfway down the list in the default zoom). Use the ... next to the dropdown to see all the available colors.

(To get back to the default color choose Text Black for the standard Access theme.)

## Change the Font in a Text Box

These instructions are for changing the font in a specific text box. See the next chapter for changing the fonts used in all forms and reports at once.

To change the font used for a particular label or text box, click into the text box, go to the Font section of the Format tab, and select a different font from the dropdown menu.

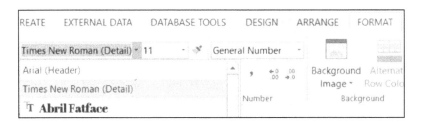

You can also use the Text Formatting section of the Home tab.

Or you can go to the Font Name row in the Property Sheet (a little less than halfway down) and choose a new font from there.

To change all of the label and text boxes in that one form or report to a different font, use Ctrl + A to select all text boxes first and then make your change. For forms, you'll need to use the Format or

Home tabs to make that change, not the Property sheet. Same for reports in Layout View.

If you do select more than one label or text box at a time, the dropdown menu for Font may look blank before you make your choice, but that's okay. That's just because the selected text boxes are using more than one font and so it shows as blank since it can't show multiple fonts at once. When you select your new font then that will apply to all selected text boxes regardless of the font they were using previously.

## Change the Font Size in a Text Box

My version of Access defaults to an 11 pt font size, but I've found that using an 8 pt font size makes it easier for me to fit all of my data onto one report page so I do this one often.

To change font size you can go to the Font section of the Format tab or the Text Formatting section of the Home tab and select a new font size from the dropdown menu on the right of the font menu. You can also type in the font size you want instead of using the dropdown.

Or you can go to the Font Size option on the Property Sheet (about midway down the list) and change the value there.

Once more, if you select all text boxes in your form or report your best bet is to use the Format tab or Home tab. Selecting more than one text box may mean the dropdown menu is blank until you make your selection.

## Unselect Text Boxes

This is a good point to tell you how to unselect text boxes you've selected because Esc doesn't work in Access the way it does in some of the other programs. The easiest way I've found to unselect text boxes I don't want selected is to just click into a blank space somewhere in the form or report workspace.

## Change the Text in a Label Text Box

If you need to change the text in a *label* text box, you have a couple of options.

You can double-click on the label box until you see your cursor within that box and then you can replace the text by typing in your new text and deleting the old text.

Or you can change the entry for Caption in the Property Sheet.

This is for label text boxes only. DO NOT change the text of any data text box. Because if you do so Access won't know what field to pull the information from and when you look at your form or report in Form or Report View you'll see #Name? in that field instead of your values. You may also suddenly have an Enter Parameter dialogue box popping up when you try to switch to Form or Report View.

It's absolutely fine to change the text in the *label* box for those fields, but don't change the data input text.

If you think you might do so by accident, then I would suggest you only make changes to field labels in the Property Sheet because for data input boxes there is no Caption field that you can change.

## Add Formatting to a Numeric Data Field

To apply a format to a data field in your form or report, you again have a couple of options.

In the Property Sheet for a data field the first option is Format. For data fields with numbers in them there is a dropdown menu where you can choose between General Number, Currency, Euro, Fixed, Standard, Percent, and Scientific.

(For text you won't have options to choose. The dropdown is blank.)

I tend to use Currency for monetary values which formats my numbers, because I'm in the U.S., using a $ sign and two decimal places. And I use Standard for basic numbers like units sold because it includes a comma separator for any thousands.

To give you an idea of the difference, General would show 1234.56, Currency would show $1,234.56, and Standard would show 1,234.56.

Also, the next option in the Property Sheet is Decimal Places. If I'm trying to save space I will change that to zero which will then round my values to the nearest whole number. This would return 1235, $1,235, and 1,235 in those three formats.

Your other option is the Number section of the Format tab where there is a dropdown menu that gives the same options, General Number, Currency, Euro, Fixed, Standard, Percent, and Scientific.

You can also use the Increase Decimals and Decrease Decimals options below that on the right side to change the number of decimal places that are visible.

The $ sign, % sign, and comma that are below the dropdown are just shortcut ways to change the format of a field to Currency, Percent, and Standard, respectively.

The Number section will be grayed out if a field you are clicked into is not formatted as a number field.

## Change Formatting for a Date Field

By default, Access adds a date field to the top of any report and the date format it uses is Long Date which includes day of the week and a spelled out version of the date. Access also has a field right below that with the Long Time which shows hour, minute, and seconds. I usually delete the time field because it's not important for my reports to have that level of detail. And I like to change the format of the date field.

To change the date format, click on the field, go to the Number section of the Format tab, and in the dropdown that says Long Date, choose a different option from General Date, Medium Date, or Short Date.

You can also go to the Property Sheet and choose your option from the dropdown for the Format field.

I tend to prefer General Date or Short Date for my own reports, but if I were working with an international team I'd probably choose Medium Date since it solves any potential question of whether 3/2/2020 is March 2nd or February 3rd since that can vary depending on what country you're in.

## Bold the Text in a Text Box

If you want the text within a text box to be bolded, you can click on the box you want to edit and use Ctrl + B.

Or you can click on the box, go to the Font section of the Format tab or the Text Formatting section of the Home tab, and click on the capital B for bold there.

Or, for the largest number of options, go to the Property Sheet and change the value for Font Weight. There you have the choice of Thin, Extra Light, Light, Normal, Medium, Semi-Bold, Bold, Extra Bold, and Heavy.

To undo bolding of your text, use Ctrl + B, click on the B option in one of the tabs, or change the value in the Property Sheet to Normal. (If you chose a bolding option in the Property Sheet and try to use Ctrl + B to remove it, you may have to use Ctrl + B twice for it to work.)

## Italicize Text in a Text Box

If you want to italicize the text in a text box, select that box, and use Ctrl + I.

You can also click on the slanted I in the Font section of the Format tab or the Text Formatting section of the Home tab.

Or you can change the setting for Font Italic in the Property Sheet to Yes.

To remove italics, use Ctrl + I, click on the slanted I in one of the tabs, or change the Font Italic setting to No in the Property Sheet.

## Underline Text in a Text Box

Note that this is different from adding a solid line under a text box, which would be a gridline.

To underline the text in a text box, you can use Ctrl + U.

You can also click on the underlined U in the Font section of the Format tab or the Text Formatting section of the Home tab.

Or you can change the Font Underline setting to Yes in the Property Sheet.

(Note that you only have one the single line underline option available in Access.)

To remove underlining from text, use Ctrl + U, click on the underline U in the tabs, or change the Font Underline setting to No in the Property Sheet.

## Change Text Alignment in a Text Box

By default your text boxes are going to be left-aligned, meaning the values line up with the left-hand side of their text box. But you can change this so that the values are centered or right-aligned instead. (I tend to center my numeric values, for example. I think they're easier to read that way.)

To change your text alignment, go to the Font section of the Format tab or the Text Formatting section of the Home tab, and click on the alignment option you want. They should be directly under the dropdown for font size. You have left-aligned on the left, centered in the middle, and right-aligned on the right. Each option shows a few lines and how they will look under that option.

You can also go to the Property Sheet and choose from the Text Align dropdown menu. Your options there are General, Left, Center, Right, and Distribute. I'd recommend against using Distribute unless you have a good reason for doing so.

I was also able to use a Ctrl shortcut to center my text (Ctrl + E), but I wouldn't recommend it because it looks like Access also uses that same Ctrl shortcut for a different capability in the online version. A quick glance didn't show this usage of that Ctrl shortcut as an official one for Access.

## "Wrap Text"

In Excel if you wanted all of the text information in a cell visible you'd wrap text so that it carried over onto the next line within that cell instead of being hidden after the text reached the edge of the cell. Access doesn't really have that option.

For text boxes that display your detail results, there is a Can Grow option at the very bottom of the Property Sheet that is generally set to Yes by default. It will change the height of the text box in order to display the full text of your result.

For your column headers, though, this doesn't exist as an option, so you have to manually adjust the text box height when building your table. You can force part of your text in a label text box onto a new row by using Shift + Enter instead of just Enter.

If you have a text box in a report that shows summary data there is a Can Grow option in the Property Sheet, but I'd recommend there just changing the height of the text box if the results look a little squished.

## Delete a Text Box

If you want to delete a text box that's currently in your form or report, you can click on that text box, right-click, and choose Delete from the dropdown menu. For Forms this will delete both the label and the data text box. For Reports it will just delete the text box you clicked on.

This means that sometimes the Delete Row or Delete Column option will be the better choice, but just be sure that you're only deleting what you want to delete if you use one of those options.

You can also click onto a text box and use the Delete option from your keyboard. Or you can use the Delete option in the Records section of the Home tab.

## Add a Text Box From Your Source Data

To add a text box to your form or report that is from the source you're using to build the form or report, go to the Design tab and click on Add Existing Fields. This will show you a pane on the right-hand side with the name of all fields available from that source. You can then left-click on the field name you want and drag it into your form or report in the location you want to add it.

Fields come into a form or report in a stacked layout, meaning with the label on the left-hand side and then the value on the right. You can change this under the Arrange tab by choosing Tabular from the Table section. That will change the field display so that the label is in a header row and the values are listed below it.

If you add a new text box and change it to Tabular, it will not be tied to the other text boxes in that row and so will not automatically move with them or resize with them.

## Change the Positioning of a Text Box

You can move your text boxes around within your form or report. Often I need to do this after I've added a new text box or deleted ones I didn't want.

In Layout View you can left-click onto the boxes you want to move and drag them to the new location. Just be aware that the label box and the text box with your data in it may move separately, so if that happens you will need to select both of them (using Ctrl) before you drag if you want to keep them together.

In Design View you can also click and drag, but I'll warn you now it's a little finicky and may take a try or two to get your fields where you want them.

Sometimes in Design View you can click and drag on a text box and it won't move at all. In that case you may need to click on the box in the top right corner that shows four arrows in order to move that text box and any other associated text boxes.

Clicking onto that box with the four-sided arrow in it will make sure that your text box moves, but it may also move other text boxes with it. When your data is in columns, this is generally good because it moves the label box as well as any summary box that's associated with your data. But when I was playing with this I found in one instance where it would move three data text boxes and their labels together as a group when I only wanted to move the one.

In that case, which was in a form, in order to reorder those text boxes, I had to click on the data text box for the field that interested me and move it. The label text box automatically moved as well. But I couldn't use the four-sided arrow box at the corner of the label box.

So, basically, you can just click into the data text box you want to move, try it, see what happens and then adjust from there by going back and selecting the label box as well if the label didn't move or by using the four-sided arrow box in the top left corner if the text box won't move at all.

Another way I've found to reposition some text boxes that don't want to move for me is to change the size of the text box instead. So if there's room I'll stretch the text box to where I want it to be on the left or right edge, whichever direction I'm trying to move, and then I'll bring the other side over or change the Width setting on the Property Sheet to what I want it to be.

# FORMS AND REPORTS:
# EDITING AND FORMATTING AT THE DOCUMENT LEVEL

We just talked about a number of edits you can make at the level of the text entries in your form or report, but there is other formatting that we need to discuss as well. That's the type of formatting that can happen to the overall form or report.

* * *

### Change the Size of a Document So It Fits One Page

Often times I find that when I have Access create a report for me and then change the font size and the text box size that it will still carry over to another page even though there's no content left to carry over to that page.

I always fix this in Design View. What you can do there is put your cursor along the right-hand edge of the design space until it turns into a double-sided arrow, and then left-click and drag to the left until the document only takes up one page.

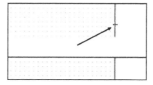

This is only possible if there aren't any text boxes in that space. Usually, that means you're going to first need to move the Page Numbering text box over to the left. You may also need to move the header, but usually it's just the page numbering that hangs over into the blank area.

## Change the Height of a Section in a Report

If you resize a text box in a section in your report to be taller that will also resize the space that entire section takes up on the page so that it fits. But if you shrink the height of a text box, it won't automatically adjust the size of that section of the report. This can lead to there being unsightly space within your report. Like so:

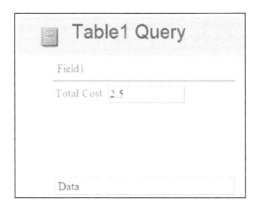

If I look in Design View I can see all that blank space that exists between the Total Cost text box and the bottom of the section.

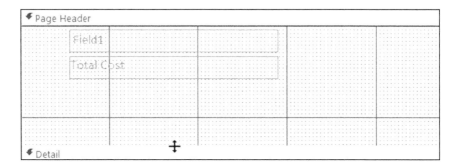

The way to fix this is to go into Design View and hold your cursor along the bottom edge for the section until you see the double-sided arrow pointing upward and downward, and to then left-click and drag until right below the closest text box.

## Page Numbering in Reports

If you use one of the methods we discussed to create your report then by default the report will have page numbering in the bottom right corner of the page.

To move your page number elsewhere in the document, treat it like you would any text box and click and drag.

If you want to use different formatting, you can instead delete the page numbering that's already in your report and replace it.

To add a new page number, go to the Header/Footer section of the Design tab, and click on Page Numbers.

This will bring up the Page Numbers dialogue box where you can choose to have the page numbers display as either Page N of M or just Page N, and where you can set the position for the page numbering as either top of page or bottom of page. You can also set whether the page number shows in the left corner, center, right corner, inside, or outside.

When you use the Page Numbers dialogue box it inserts a new page number, so if you don't delete the old one you'll have two sets of page number in your report.

Also, in my opinion, where it by default inserts page numbering on the top of the page is weird since it's below the header section which makes the first page look odd..

Use Ctrl + X and then Ctrl + V if you need to move it from one section of the report to another and it won't let you drag it. When you do so it will likely paste in on the far left-hand side of the section and then you can left-click and drag to where you want it within the section.

## Changing the Highlighted Rows in Reports

By default, Access will highlight every other row of your results in a report a light gray color. This can make it easier to distinguish values in different rows as you're reading across your document.

However, this highlighting also carries over to any group headings and summary rows you insert in your report. So, for example, in a report grouped by Author, the first author name would be a white row, the next author name would be a gray row, etc. This does not really help with reading comprehension and can look weird, so I prefer to remove it.

To remove highlighting from any section of your report, select the *section*, and then go to the Format tab, and change the Alternate Row Color dropdown to No Color. (This may mean not clicking onto a specific text box, but instead clicking into the area next to a text box.)

You can also change the color used for this highlighting by using the Alternate Row Color dropdown and selecting a color option instead of No Color.

To return to the default color used by Access choose Automatic.

You can also make this change in the Property Sheet. To do so you need to click on the bar for that section in the workspace. So where it says Page Header, [Group] Header, Detail, etc. You'll know you've made the correct selection when the Property Sheet options include a row for Back Color and one for Alternate Back Color. Change the value for Alternate Back Color to No Color to remove the lines, Automatic to use the default, or any other color (by using the …) that you want.

And if you want to go really wild (but please don't it with your Detail section) you can set colors for both Back Color and Alternate Back Color in the Property Sheet. This will color all of your rows for that section, alternating between the Back Color and Alternate Back Color you chose. If you do so, you will probably also have to change the Back Color for the text boxes in that section as well or they'll remain white while the rest of the row is colored.

## Using Themes in Forms and Reports

A quick and easy way to generate a form or report that isn't the Access default is to use themes. These are available in the Themes section of the Design tab. I have nine of them that show as options when I click on the dropdown arrow under Themes. They all come with different colors for the header section of the form or report and some also change the font.

The problem with using a theme is that it will change *all* of your forms and reports, not just the one you're working on, which can be a little unexpected and disconcerting and may impact how your forms or reports display.

## Using Colors in Forms and Reports

Another option for mixing things up is to use the Colors dropdown in the Themes section of the Design tab, which will apply a different color palette to your forms and reports.

Once again, this will happen to all of your forms and reports, not just the one you're working with.

## Assigning a New Font Family to Forms and Reports

The final option in the Themes section of the Design tab is the Fonts dropdown. This allows you to assign a different font family for use in all of your forms or reports. If you look at the dropdown you'll see that the first font listed is for the headers in the document and the second one listed is for the data entries.

For example, here I'm using Arial and Times New Roman:

You can see in the background that Apple Nov is in Arial (a sans-serif font, meaning it has no little feet at the bottom of the letters) and the field names and values are in Times New Roman (a serif font that does have little feet at the base of the letters like you see with the N in November.)

## Replace the Logo in a Form or Report

By default the forms and reports generated by Access include a small image in the top left corner. You can go to the Header/Footer section of the Design tab and click on Logo to select an image from your computer to use in place of this image.

Be careful, because doing so will delete the image that was already there, so that even if you undo you will not get the other image back.

If the logo you insert doesn't look right, try going to the Property Sheet and while clicked on the logo changing the Size Mode to Stretch or Zoom instead of Clip.

(I inserted a picture for my logo. It just looked like a blurred mess in Clip mode, but was stretched to a square version of the image when I used Stretch and was displayed as a rectangular image within that square space—which was what it was—when I used Zoom.)

## Controls

The Controls section of the Design tab is really for if you're building a form or report from scratch, which we're not doing here so I'm not going to walk through all of those in detail. At this level of knowledge probably the only one you might want to use is the Label option to insert text that isn't tied to a field of data anywhere. This could be useful for something like a Copyright notice or disclaimer. You just click on the option and then go to your workspace and click and drag up and over until it creates a text box. You can then type in the textbox whatever text you wanted to include.

## Stacked vs. Tabular Layout

I touched on this briefly before but there are two main types of layout for your data fields, stacked and tabular. The choice of which to use is available in the Table section of the Arrange tab. By default forms will be in a stacked format which Access describes as a "layout similar to a paper form, with labels to the left of each field." Reports by default tend to be in a tabular format which Access describes as "a layout similar to a spreadsheet, with labels across the top and data in columns below the labels."

You can easily change an entire form or report to the opposite format by using Ctrl + A to select all of your text boxes, then using Ctrl while you unselect any headers or footers, and then making your selection of Stacked or Tabular from the Arrange tab. But usually I just need this option for a new field I've added.

# REPORTS:
# REPORT SECTIONS

Okay. Now it's time to focus in on just reports because there are a few things you can do with a report that you can't do with a form. Namely, grouping, sorting, and totals. But before we dig into those, we need to discuss the different sections that are available in a report.

## Report Header

The report header appears at the very beginning of your report and will not repeat onto other pages if the report is more than one page long. This is where you can provide the title of the report, your company logo, etc.

You can place a summary field in the report header. If you do so, the summed value will be for the entire report.

Keep in mind that the report header is in addition to the page header, so on the first page of your report you will see them both.

## Page Header

The page header appears at the top of every single page of your report. This is a good place for column labels, for example. Or where you would put your page numbering if you had your page numbering at the top of your report. Access also suggests repeating the name of the report in the page header.

## Group Header

If you choose to group your data within your report, then the group header is what will show at the top of each grouping of your data. Keep in mind, that what will show are the different values within your chosen group.

So, if, for example, I group my data on Series Name, then the name of each of my series will be shown in my group header before the report lists detailed information for that group.

You can have a calculated value in your group header. If you do, the calculated value will be for that group and that group only.

You can also have multiple group headers in a report. For example, I have a report that shows profit and loss where the high-level grouping is for type of book (non-fiction, mystery, etc.) and then below that I have another grouping for each category within that type. So my Non-Fiction grouping has categories below that for Computers, Business/Compliance, Budgeting, etc.

When you have multiple groupings, you can have multiple summaries. So, for example, I can have one overall summary for profit and loss for all of my non-fiction titles and then another summary for just those related to computers.

## Detail

Detail is where the most granular level of information is displayed. In the report I mentioned above I have groupings for non-fiction as well as each type of non-fiction, and then under each type of non-fiction, for example, Computers, I have listed each series name (Excel Essentials, Word Essentials, etc.) and information related to units sold, revenue, ad cost, production cost, and profit/loss for each of those series.

I could have just as easily had my detail section be each title that is related to computers instead of each series. What you choose to put in the detail section is up to you and what you want your report to do.

## Group Footer

The group footer is much like the group header except it comes at the end of the group's detail data. This is generally where I include my summary values rather than in the header. As above, you can have as many group footers as there are groupings of your data. Any summary value will be for that grouping level.

## Page Footer

The page footer is what's displayed at the bottom of every single page of your report. This is usually where I have my page numbering. You could also have any copyright notice or other disclaimer you felt needed to be on each page.

## Report Footer

The report footer is only shown on the last page. This is where you can put a total value for the entire report, for example. Any summary value in the report footer will sum values for all groups in the report.

If you look in Design View the report footer shows after the page footer, but that's just in Design View. When the report is actually viewed in Report View or printed, the page footer will be the last thing on the last page and the report footer will come at the end of your data somewhere in the main portion of the page.

* * *

Here is the Design View for a report I use of Lifetime Profit and Loss By Genre with Category Detail that gives you a good view of the different sections.

This is a report derived from a query that contains all of the information necessary to generate the report.

You can see that the Report Header in this report is the report name and the date it was printed. That only appears on the first page.

Next is the Page Header which shows the columns names for the data in the Detail section. (If I were to move those column names down, then they would repeat at each grouping level they'd been moved to. As it's set now they just show at the top of each printed page.)

After that is my first Group Header. As you can see Access names each group for the field being used to create the group. In this case it shows as my Genre Header. This is where I list the genre/type of book. For example, Non-Fiction or Mystery.

Right after that is another Group Header. This one for Category. These are for the subsets within that genre/type. For example, Computers for Non-Fiction or Cozy for Mystery.

And then we have the Detail section. That's where all of the actual detailed data is shown. In this case I'm showing results by related series. And providing units, revenue, ad cost, production cost, and profit/loss for each series.

After that is the first Group Footer, this one for Category so that's why it's named the Category Footer. You can see that we're taking the sum of the values from the detail section for each category.

And then the next Group Footer, this one for Genre. We're also taking a total for all fields at this level. This will give the total units, revenues, etc. for each genre/type.

Then you can see the Page Footer. This is what shows at the bottom of every page of the report. It's just the page number and it's set up to be "Page X of Y".

And then finally you have a Report Footer which will show totals for all of those fields for all of the data listed in the report, regardless of group. (Keep in mind that while this shows last in Design View, the totals will actually appear directly below the total values for the last grouping in the report.)

You can see how the structure is sort of a sandwich moving from highest-level to most detailed level and back out again. As you move in from top and bottom the layers match one another. So the outmost layers are report header/footer, followed by page header/footer, etc.

* * *

One nice thing to know about the different sections of the report is that as you group or total your data these sections tend to be added for you. You don't have to try to create them yourself. You just have to understand how they work so that you can make edits where you need to.

Okay. So let's talk about Grouping, Sorting, and Totaling your data now.

# REPORTS:
## GROUPING YOUR DATA

I'd say at least half of the reports I use have my data grouped on at least one level and sometimes more than one level. For example, I have a report of Profit and Loss By Author with Series Detail. That one has one level of grouping by each author name. But I could as easily have it show title-level detail, too, and group at the series level as well.

Grouping is just a nice way to organize and present data.

### Layout View

The easiest way to do this is probably in Layout View.

Open the report that you want to add a grouping level to in Layout View.

Right-click on the label for the field you want to use for your grouping, and choose "Group On [Field Name]" from the dropdown.

This will move that field to the left-hand side and you'll see that your report is now grouped on that field name.

You should also see a Group, Sort, and Total section appear at the bottom of the workspace that shows that you've grouped your report on that field.

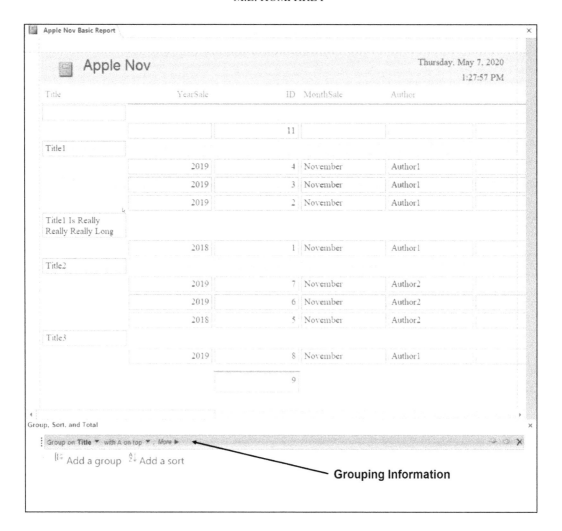

* * *

That's one way to group your fields.

Another is to open your report in Layout View and then click on Group & Sort in the Grouping & Totals section of the Design tab.

This will make the Group, Sort, and Total section visible below your report.

Click on Add a Group and then choose the field you want to group on from the dropdown menu.

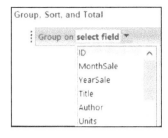

\* \* \*

To add another level of grouping, just do the same thing again. If your report is currently grouped on Field A and then Field B and you want to reverse that so that you group on Field B first, you can use the up and down arrows on the right-hand side of the Group, Sort, and Total workspace to change which grouping is performed first.

When you have multiple levels of grouping, each subsequent grouping level is only made within the prior groupings levels. So if I group by author first and each author only writes one type of book, then grouping by type of book underneath that does nothing. Because under each name there's only one type of book. But reverse that and group by type first and then if I have multiple authors who write that type of book, the two levels of grouping actually separate out my information better.

\* \* \*

To delete a level of grouping, you can go into the Group, Sort, and Total section and click on the X on the right-hand side of the workspace next to that group.

\* \* \*

Each grouping comes with a default sort order as well as other default choices. You can see all of them by clicking on More in the Group, Sort, and Total section. Like so:

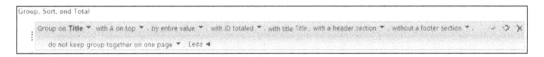

Each one can be changed by clicking on the arrows to see the available options in a dropdown menu. The one I usually need to edit is the "do not keep together on one page" option at the end. I like to change this option so that I can keep the header and the first record of each group on the same page.

\* \* \*

## Design View

You can also group your records in Design View.

To do so, open your report in Design View. Right-click on the field you want to group on, and choose Group On from the dropdown menu.

Your results will be grouped by that field and you will now have a Group Header section for that group, but there will be no field in the header section. The data will just have spaces between each grouping but the actual values for the group you chose will remain in the detail section like in this example where I've chosen to group on Author:

You can cut and paste the text box for that field from the Details section to the Title Header section if you want the value to be shown in the title header section but not in the detail section. (If you do so, be sure to also delete the associate label text box from the Page Header section.

I will warn you that cutting and pasting works a little strangely with this one. Cut is fine, but then paste seems like it won't work because you can't select the area below Title Header. But if you just click around that are and then use Ctrl + V it will usually paste in.

Your other option is to add a new text box into the Group Header section using the Controls options under the Design tab. (Click on the Text Box option, go to the header section, click and drag up and over to create a text box, and then type into that text box the field name for the field you're grouping on. Also delete the associated label box that Access created at the same time.) This gives you a value in the header section but also values in the detail section.

Like so where I have the Title field in both the detail section and group header:

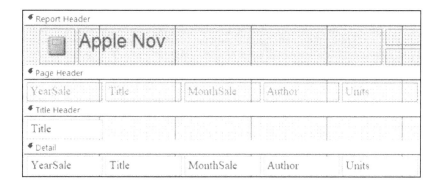

Which looks like this in the report:

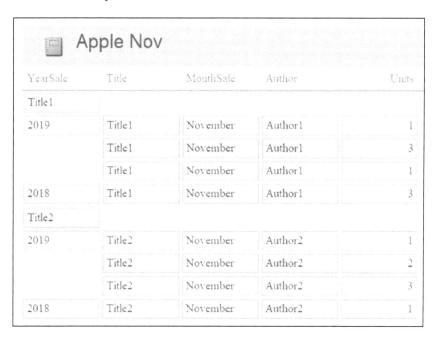

The Group, Sort, and Total section in Design View works generally the same way as it does in Layout View. You can add a grouping from there, too, but it will have that same Design View issue where there is no field in the group header section.

# REPORTS:
# SORTING YOUR DATA

As we've touched on a bit above, you can also sort your report by any of your data fields.

## Group, Sort, and Totals Section

The easiest way to do this is pull up the Group, Sort, and Totals section if it isn't already visible, and click on Add a Sort.

Just like with grouping, you'll be given a list of field names to choose from. Select the one you want to sort on. The default will be to sort in ascending order (from A to Z, from smallest to largest, etc.), but you can click on that arrow for that option and change it to sort in descending order instead.

You can also choose how many characters to sort for text or to sort on an interval for numbers. (I find this one odd and can't see when I'd use it but I'm sure someone has at some point in time.) The default is to sort on the entire value.

Clicking on the More option will allow you to group your data if desired.

You can add more than one level of sorting to your report, just keep in mind that the first level will always be the dominant sort order. So if I, for example, sort by ID there's no point in sorting on anything else because my ID field is unique.

Also note that for sorts there's nothing in your report that will indicate the sort order you're using. You can usually identify it visually.

## Layout View

In Layout View you can right-click on a field you want to sort by and choose your sort option. Both the ascending and descending options for that field type will be available to choose from.

When you do add a sort this way it will also appear in the Group, Sort, and Totals section down below.

The right-click on a field in Layout View option only works if you want to sort by one field, not multiple fields. When I tried to add a second field to the sort by right-clicking on a different field and choosing a sort order, it overwrote the sort for the first one.

## Design View

In Design View you can also right-click on a field you want to sort by and choose your sort option from the dropdown menu, but again it only works if you want to sort by one field. Your sort will also appear in the Group, Sort, and Totals section.

* * *

If you're both grouping and sorting your data, pay attention to the order in which you group and sort. If you have, for example, a sort on units before you have a grouping on author name, then the sort on the number of units will take precedence over the grouping on author name making the grouping probably useless. But if you put the grouping first then the data would group on author name and sort on units only after that had happened.

Remember, you can use the up and down arrows in the Group, Sort, and Total workspace to change the order of your groups and sorts.

Also, in case you run into this issue, if you ever try to sort on a summed value that you've added to your report, that isn't possible using the sorting options as we've just walked through them. You'd need to have those sums in the query or table that you pull from for the report to sort on them.

# REPORTS:
# ADD SUMMARY VALUES

Speaking of sums, let's talk about how you add totals to your report.

I like to get all my groups in order first. Once you have that, it's pretty straight-forward.

## Layout View

Click onto the label for the field where you want to add a totals value. Then go to the Grouping & Totals section of the Design tab, click on the dropdown arrow next to Totals, and choose the summary type you want to use. I almost exclusively use Sum. But your other options are Average, Count Records, Count Values, Max, Min, Standard Deviation, and Variance.

You can also right-click on the field name to bring up the dropdown menu, then go to Total [Field Name], and then choose your summation option from the secondary dropdown menu.

(Just a word of warning that if you're going to mix and match these and have a sum for one and a count for another, for example, you really need to find a way to properly label those results so it's clear what summation value is being provided for each field.)

When you add a summary value, if you already have your groupings in place then you will get a summation at every level of grouping that you had in your report.

So here I've added a sum of units in a report that's grouped at the Title and Year level.

| Title | YearSale | MonthSale | Author | Units |
|-------|----------|-----------|--------|-------|
| **Apple Nov** | | | | |
| Title1 | | | | |
| | 2018 | | | |
| | | November | Author1 | 3 |
| | | | | 3 |
| | 2019 | | | |
| | | November | Author1 | 1 |
| | | November | Author1 | 3 |
| | | November | Author1 | 1 |
| | | | | 5 |
| | | | | 8 |

When I chose Totals for the Units field Access added total values for each year as well as each title. If I were to scroll to the bottom of the report I would also have an overall total for all titles for all years.

If you don't group first, Access will not automatically add summary values for the new grouping levels.

## Design View

In Design View, you can click onto either the label text box or the data text box for the field you want to summarize and then click on your choice from the Totals dropdown in the Grouping & Totals section of the Design tab. Like above, if your data has already been grouped, this will add a summary field at every level.

And, just like above, if you add your totals first and then group, they will not carry through to your new group levels.

You can also right-click on the field you want to total, go to Total in the dropdown menu, and then choose your totals option in the secondary dropdown. Note that in this case the option in the dropdown menu just says Total and doesn't include the field name, too, like it does in Layout View.

## Group, Sort, and Total

If you have groups or sorts listed in the Group, Sort, and Total section, you can also go into the More options for that group or sort and change the fourth option to say which field you want to count or sum related to that group or sort. If you want more than one summation for that field you'll have to keep going in there to check both options you want and if there's more than one grouping you'll have to do it for each group separately.

But this option does also let you choose to show what percent of the total is represented by the value in each group.

As you choose different fields they will add to this section so you can make these choices for more than one field.

\* \* \*

By default Access is going to use a gridline with your different totals fields. You may want to also change the font, bold, or italics for the field to further distinguish it from your detail numbers. I also sometimes add a little extra space in Design View for the totals values to set them apart from my main data. And I often find that the totals text boxes need to be resized to effectively show their values. They're generally too short for some reason.

# REPORTS:
# CONDITIONAL FORMATTING

Conditional formatting lets you add bolding, italics, underline, a different font color, or a different fill color to a text box if certain criteria are met.

I'll confess that this isn't something I had used in Access before, but I added it to some of my reports after testing it out and it's pretty straightforward to use if you are already familiar with conditional formatting in Excel.

So. Let's walk through this.

In either Layout View or Design View, click into the data portion of the field where you want to have your conditional formatting applied. (So in Layout View, click on one of the entries. In Design View click on the data text box for that field.)

You'll know you've done this correctly when you go to the Format tab and under the Control Formatting section the Conditional Formatting option is available to you and not grayed out.

Click on it to bring up the Conditional Formatting Rules Manager dialogue box.

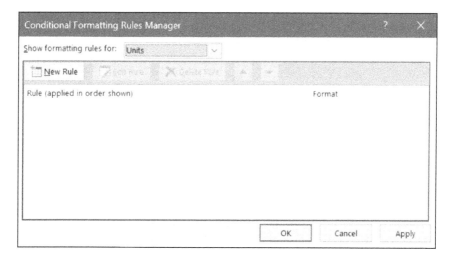

Click on New Rule to add a new rule. If you already have rules in place you'll also be able to click on Edit Rule and Delete Rule.

You have two choices, "check values in the current record or use an expression" or "compare to other records".

To build a simple rule that formats values greater than a set amount, keep the first option (check values) selected, and then set your criteria and your formatting in the section down below.

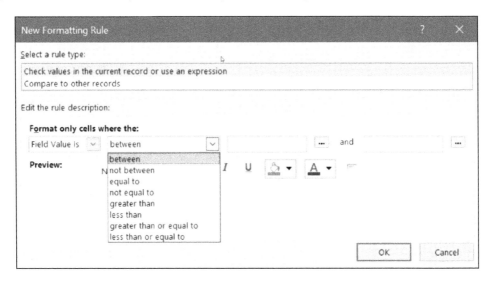

So if I want to bold all values in a field that are greater than 10, I would choose "Field Value Is", "Greater Than", and then type in 10. Below that I would then click on the B to bold the text.

Rather than add a set value you can also click on the … and add an expression that is built off of fields in your database.

The compare to other records option allows you to add data bars to your report to visually flag your records. You can do so for lowest to highest value, absolute values, or based on percentages. (Top 10%, etc.)

Here is one where I let it use the default color and create data bars for lowest to highest values:

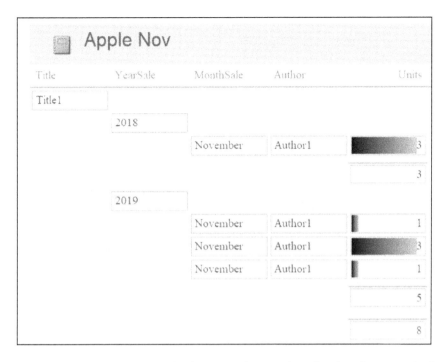

You can see that when the units were the largest value, 3, that the data bar was the longest. And when the units were the lowest value, 1, the data bar was the shortest.

When you've made all of your selections, click OK, and then click OK again to go back to your report.

You can go back in to edit or delete an existing rule the same way you went in to create a new one, just be sure that you have the correct field selected when looking for an existing rule. If you don't, you can always change the field name in the dropdown menu at the top of the Conditional Formatting Rules Manager dialogue box.

To edit or delete a rule, click on it and then choose Edit Rule or Delete Rule.

You can have more than one rule apply to a field. The order in which they appear will dictate which rule is applied first. The order can be the difference between a rule working and not, so if a rule you create doesn't seem to be running, check for rule order.

Also, I was able to apply the check values formatting option to a summary field by clicking on the summary field before I built the rule, but I wasn't able to apply the compare to other records option. Access acted like it would work, but then didn't show the data bars I'd supposedly added. YMMV.

# PRINT PREVIEW

I've touched on this before, but this is a good time to remind you that you should always print preview documents that you want to print from Access. I have had far too many times when a form or report looked horrible in printed form to not do this each and every time.

Reports have Print Preview built in as a View option. So you can just go to View in the Design or Home tab and select Print Preview from there. Or right-click in the workspace and choose Print Preview from the dropdown menu.

Forms do not have Print Preview built in as a View option so you need to go to the File tab, choose Print on the left-hand side, and then choose Print Preview that way.

Whichever way you get there it will then show you a preview of your form or report as it will print. You will also have options under the Page Size and Page Layout sections of the Print Preview tab to change your page size, margins, and page orientation (portrait or landscape).

(The Zoom section options just let you change how the print preview shows in your workspace. The Data section options allow you to export the document rather than print it.)

The arrows at the bottom of the print preview workspace let you move through the document one printed page at a time.

Always, always check for fields that continue on to the next page so you can go back and fix those.

Also, remember that narrowing your margins or changing the orientation may easily fix a form or report that carries over onto a second page.

To print a document double-sided, you need to choose to Print and then click on Properties in the Print dialogue box. Usually if you make that choice once it will save for the next time you choose to print that document.

# OTHER TIPS AND TRICKS

A few more random tidbits to share with you:

## Refresh Data

I often find myself working back and forth between a few data tables and a query or report to get the query or report working properly. Sometimes this requires making an update to my data. (For example, to list an identifier in my master table that was missing.)

When I have a query or report already open and I make an update like that to a data table that is feeding into the query or report, the query or report does not automatically update. To get it to update I need to use the Refresh All option in the Records section of the Home tab. This refresh the data in your query or report without you having to close it and reopen it.

If you still have the data table open, sometimes the refresh won't work. So be sure to close the data table before you Refresh All.

## Compact & Repair

I'll admit, I don't do this probably near as much as I should, but you should periodically compact and repair your database. It will clean up space that's being used that doesn't need to be and may improve performance.

To do this, go to the File tab and then choose Compact & Repair.

I just did this on the database I was using to write these books. It was 2 MB before I ran it and 1 MB after. So doing so halved the size of my database. I also just did it on my database I use regularly where I've gone through recently and changed some field names and it went from 32 MB to 10 MB.

So if size or performance is an issue, well worth doing. (You can also Compact & Repair from the Database Tools tab under the Tools section.)

## Export to PDF

If you want to send a report from Access to another user via email, exporting that report to a PDF file is probably an easy way to do so.

To export a report (or table or query or form) to a PDF, select it, go to the External Data tab, and choose PDF or XPS under the Export section. This will bring up a Publish as PDF or XPS dialogue box. Choose where you want it to save, rename it if you need to, and then click on Publish.

Keep in mind that the document you generate in PDF format will have the same issues that you'd have in printing from Access, which is why I would generally only use this for a well-formatted form or report that has already been checked in Print Preview.

## Find

Access does have a find and a replace function just like in other Office programs. I'd be very leery of using the replace portion of it given the way changes to data stick in Access, but find can be a handy way for locating a specific record.

You have a few options here. You can open your table, query, form, or report and then click on the binoculars that say Find in the Find section of the Home tab. This will bring up the Find dialogue box for reports or queries or the Find and Replace dialogue box for tables and forms.

Type in what you want to find in the Find What field on the Find tab and then choose where you want to look. If you just want to look in a specific field you need to be clicked into it before you open the dialogue box.

It appears from my testing that the find will only work on detailed data entries. It doesn't seem to work on group headings or labels. This can be particularly useful to know if you are building a large report and wanted to search on a field that you're making into a group header. In that case you may want to duplicate your data and leave that value in a column in the detail section as well.

You can also use Ctrl + F to bring up the Find or the Find and Replace dialogue box.

## AutoCorrect

I've yet to run into this because for the most part I upload my data into Access rather than adding new entries directly in Access, but it turns out that Access has an AutoCorrect feature which will change your data entries on you. If you immediately notice that it's done so, you can use Ctrl + Z to change the entry back. But it's probably an even better idea if you're using your database for direct entry to turn AutoCorrect off entirely.

To do so, click on the File tab, and then click on Options on the left-hand side. From there click on Proofing and then on the AutoCorrect Options button. Uncheck the box for "Replace Text as You Type" to turn off all AutoCorrect. And then click OK and OK again.

## Change Navigation Pane Options

One last tip. This is something I've never needed, but I did accidentally trigger it at one point and I could see how it might be useful under certain circumstances.

What I call the All Access Objects pane is what Access calls the Navigation Pane. This is the pane that is on the left-hand side of the screen. It can be minimized, but it can't be closed.

By default it shows all of your tables, queries, forms, and reports in that order with the objects in each category then listed alphabetically.

But it turns out you can change this.

If you left-click on the gray arrow next to All Access Objects you will see a dropdown menu of choices:

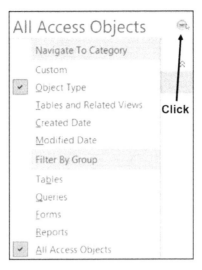

The Tables and Related Views choice will rearrange the pane so that each table is shown with its associated queries, forms, and reports listed underneath like you see here for Table1:

The Created Date option will group your objects by when they were created. The database I've been using for these books shows with Last Week, Two Weeks Ago, and Older as the categories. So this is probably an easy way to see what has been added to a database recently.

The Modified Date option will group your objects by when they were last modified. My categories for this one are showing the days of this week from Sunday onward, Last Week, Two Weeks Ago, and Older. So a good way to check what tables, queries, forms, or reports have been recently modified.

Below those choices is a grayed in header that reads Filter By Group. And below that are the groupings available for your given selection. So with Object Type as the view we had Tables, Queries, Forms, and Reports and I could click on just one to show only that category type. With Tables and Related Views I had the individual table names.

The bottom option each time will be an All [X] option that you can click to show all of the objects, tables, or dates, depending on the display choice you made in the top section.

# WHERE TO GO FROM HERE

Alright, so that's all we're going to cover here.

There are still things that I haven't covered about Access. My goal with these books was to provide you the information I think you need but in manageable chunks.

At this point most of what I haven't covered is information I don't think you'll use much. Like how to have a hyperlink field or to use Access to create a web app. Or how to split your Access database when it's a shared database. And some of the topics are just way more advanced than the average user needs to know, like using macros and Visual Basic.

But you may need to know about one of those topics one day. So how do you find the answers?

Access help is a great place to start. You can click on the question mark in the top right corner to bring up the Access Help dialogue box and search from there.

I also think that the Microsoft website is incredibly helpful. I usually get there by doing an internet search and including microsoft in the search terms so that one of my first search results will link to the support.office.com or the microsoft.com websites. When doing this keep in mind that at the top of every help topic they show which versions of Access the article applies to, like this one called *Introduction to Reports in Access*:

Introduction to reports in Access

*Access for Microsoft 365, Access 2019, Access 2016, Access 2013, Access 2010, Access 2007*

See the line directly below that that lists the various Access iterations it covers.

And, of course, there's a general internet search. Most problems you encounter will not be new ones. Someone out there has tried to figure out how to do the same thing you are and you can search for those questions and answers to find the solution. Or, if you're brave, you can ask the question yourself on one of the many, many user forums that exist for these types of questions. Just try to be as detailed as possible when doing so about what version of Access you're using.

You can also contact me. Although I'll warn you that since I approach Access as an Excel user rather than a database developer that a lot of what I haven't covered at this point is parts of Access I simply don't use. I can look up an answer for you and provide a link, but if you're trying to implement the table analyzer or the database documenter that's just not something I'll have any experience with personally. But I'll try to help you the best I can.

# CONCLUSION

Alright. So that's it. That's *Intermediate Access*. At this point you should be able to comfortably work in most basic Access databases or create one yourself.

Remember when working in Access (or any Office program) that it has a certain underlying logic to it. Access probably the least of all of the Office programs, but it's still there. If you know that basic structure you can guess where something will be located or how it might work. Often that's how I figure out things in Excel, Word, PowerPoint, and Access. I think, "This should be possible" and then I go looking where I think it should be in that program.

Just remember with Access to back things up before you get too involved in making changes, because it's the most delicate of the Office programs. Since everything depends on relationships and the flow of data from tables to queries, forms, and reports, Access is the easiest to break.

If you do make changes to field names or relationships or queries, double-check your existing forms and reports to make sure they're still working. Keep in mind that an unexpected parameter dialogue box is very likely an indication that a query somewhere along the line isn't pulling in a field that it needs in order to work. (That's for an unexpected parameter dialogue box, not just any parameter dialogue box.)

Access is an incredibly powerful tool. I don't know how I'd track my writing business without it. But do use it with care. Proceed slowly and check and double-check that your results make sense. Always, always have ways that you can verify that a result is what you expect it to be. This may mean keeping track of values outside of Access, or using filters to verify a data upload worked correctly.

Whatever you do, don't just trust blindly. Always check. Always ask, does this make sense? Is this what I should be seeing?

But don't let it intimidate you either. You can do this. Just slow and steady. You'll get it to work if you take the time and work it through. It's all about logic and relationships.

Alright, then. Good luck with it.

# INDEX
**(In addition to the categories listed in the Table of Contents)**

## ABOUT THE AUTHOR

M.L. Humphrey is a former stockbroker with a degree in Economics from Stanford and an MBA from Wharton who has spent close to twenty years as a regulator and consultant in the financial services industry.

You can reach M.L. at mlhumphreywriter@gmail.com or at mlhumphrey.com.

www.ingramcontent.com/pod-product-compliance
Lightning Source LLC
LaVergne TN
LVHW080100070326
832902LV00014B/2331